CONTENTS

A NEW WORLD

— 1 —
THE FIRST AMERICANS

Christopher Columbus. A contemporary portrait by Sebastiano del Piombo.

At daybreak on the morning of Friday, August 3 1492, an Italian adventurer named Christopher Columbus set sail from Spain to find a new way from Europe to Asia. His aim was to open up a shorter trade route between the two continents. In Asia, he intended to load his three small ships with silks, spices and gold, and sail back to Europe a rich man.

Columbus first sailed south to the Canary Islands. Then he turned west across the unknown waters of the mid-Atlantic Ocean. Ten weeks after leaving Spain, on the morning of October 12, he stepped ashore on the beach of a low sandy island. He named the island San Salvador – Holy Savior. Columbus believed that he had landed in the Indies, a group of

islands close to the mainland of India. For this reason he called the friendly, brown-skinned people who greeted him "los Indios" – Indians.

In fact, Columbus was not near India. It was not the edge of Asia that he had reached, but islands off the shores of a new continent. Europeans would soon name the new continent America, but for many years they went on calling its inhabitants Indians. Only recently have these first Americans been described more accurately as "native Americans" or Amerindians.

There were many different groups of Amerindians. Those north of Mexico, in what is now the United States and Canada, were scattered across the grasslands and forests in separate groups called "tribes." These tribes followed very different ways of life. Some were hunters, some were farmers. Some were peaceful, others warlike. They spoke over three hundred separate languages, some of which were as different from one another as English is from Chinese.

Europeans called America "the New World." But it was not new to the Amerindians. Their ancestors had already been living there for maybe 50,000 years when Columbus stepped on to the beach in San Salvador.

We say "maybe" because nobody is completely sure. Scientists believe that the distant ancestors of the Amerindians came to America from Asia. This happened, they say, during the earth's last ice age, long before people began to make written records.

At that time a bridge of ice joined Asia to America across what is now the Bering Strait. Hunters from Siberia crossed this bridge into Alaska. From Alaska the hunters moved south and east across America, following herds of caribou and buffalo as the animals went from one feeding ground to the next. Maybe 12,000 years ago, descendants of these first Americans were crossing the isthmus of Panama into

A
HI

WITHDRAWN

Bryn O'Callaghan

Longman

Addison Wesley Longman Limited,
Edinburgh Gate, Harlow,
Essex CM20 2JE, England
and Associated Companies throughout the world.

© Longman Group UK Limited 1990

First published 1990
Eighth impression 1997

British Library Cataloguing in Publication Data
O'Callaghan, D.B. (Dennis Brynley), 1931-
An illustrated history of the U.S.A.
1. United States, history
I. Title
973

Set in 10/12 pt Bembo

Printed in China
EPC/08

ISBN 0 582 74921 2

Acknowledgements

We are grateful to the following for permission to reproduce copyright
material:
Authors' Agents for the poem ''The Dream Deferred'' by Langston Hughes
from *The Panther and the Lash – poems of our times* & Warner/Chappell Music,
Inc for portions of the lyric *With God On Our Side* by Bob Dylan, © 1963
Warner Bros Inc.

The quotation on page 98 is by M. Shulimson.

We are grateful to the following for permission to reproduce copyright
photographs and other illustrative material:

P. 4 The Metropolitan Museum of Art. Gift of Pierpont Morgan, 1900; p. 5
The Buffalo Hunt, no. 40, by Charles M. Russell, o/c, c. 1919. Amon Carter
Museum, Fort Worth; p. 7 (T) The Denver Public Library, Western History
Department, painting by Karl Bodmer; p. 7 (B) *Haida Indian Potlatch*, 1974.
Mort Künstler, Favell Museum, Klamath Falls, Oregon; p. 8 *Leiv Eiriksson
Discovering America*, by Christian Krohg, o/c 313 × 470cm.
Nasjonalgalleriet, Oslo; p. 9 The Granger Collection, New York; p. 10
United States Capital Historical Society; p. 11 From *The Story of America*, by
Louis Heren. Published by Times Books, 1976; p. 12 'Jamestown-
Yorktown Foundation Photo'; p. 13 The Granger Collection, New York; p.
14 (T) Imperial Tobacco Limited; p. 14 (B) Painting by Richard Schlecht, ©
National Geographic Society; p. 17 Peter Newark's American Pictures; p.
18 (T) The Thomas Gilcrease Institute of American History and Art, Tulsa,
Oklahoma; p.18 (B) 'Courtesy of The New-York Historical Society', New
York; p. 19 © J.L.G. Ferris, Archives of 76, Bay Village, Ohio; p. 20 (L)
From *History of the English Speaking Peoples*. Published by Macdonald & Co.
(Publishers) Limited, 1976; p. 20–21 Library Company of Philadelphia; p.
22 *Daniel Boone*, 1984. Mort Künstler, Hammer Galleries, New York; p. 23
The Metropolitan Museum of Art. Gift of Edgar William and Bernice
Chrysler Garbisch, 1963; p. 24 'Courtesy of the Royal Ontario Museum',
Toronto, Canada; p. 26 (T) 'Courtesy of the John Carter Brown Library at
Brown University'; p. 26 (B) The Granger Collection, New York; p. 27
The Metropolitan Museum of Art. Gift of Mrs Russell Sage, 1909; p. 28 Gift
of Bela J. Ward and H. Judd Ward. Collection of the Albany Institute of
History and Art; p. 29 The Granger Collection, New York; p. 30 *Reading
The Declaration of Independence To The Troops*, 1975. Mort Künstler, Federal
Hall National Memorial, New York; p. 31 Lauros-Giraudon; p. 32 New
York State Historical Association, Cooperstown; p. 33 From *Roosevelt and
the United States*, by D.B. O'Callaghan. Published by Longman, 1966; p. 34
The Metropolitan Museum of Art. Gift of Edgar William and Bernice
Garbisch, 1963; p. 36 Peter Newark's American Pictures; p. 37 Woolaroc
Museum, Bartlesville, Oklahoma; p. 38 'Courtesy of the Rhode Island
Historical Society'; p. 39 The Granger Collection, New York; p. 40 From *A
History of the Republic*, by J. West Davidson and Mark H. Lyttle. Published
by Prentice-Hall Inc., 1986; p. 41 Peter Newark's American Pictures; p. 42
Setting Traps for Beaver, by Alfred Jacob Miller. Joslyn Art Museum,
Omaha, Nebraska; p. 43 Peter Newark's American Pictures; pp. 44–46 The
Granger Collection, New York; p. 48 *Dred Scott*, by Louis Schultze, o/c.
Courtesy of the Missouri Historical Society (Neg no. S-126E); p. 49 *The
Underground Railroad*, by Charles T. Webber. Cincinnati Art Museum; p. 50
Bettmann/Hulton Picture Company; p. 52 Anne S.K. Brown Military
Collection, Brown University Library; p. 53 Fototeca Storica Nazionale
Snc.; p. 54 Bettmann/Hulton Picture Company; p. 56 The Granger
Collection, New York; p. 57 Bettmann/Hulton Picture Company; pp. 58,
59 Peter Newark's American Pictures; p. 60 *The Golden Spike*, 1985. Mort
Künstler, collection of the artist; p. 61 The Thomas Gilcrease Institute of
American History and Art, Tulsa Oklahoma; p. 62 Peter Newark's
American Pictures; p. 63 (T) *Across the Continent. "Westward the Course of
Empire Takes its Way"*, by Fanny Palmer, toned lithograph (hand colored),
1868. Amon Carter Museum, Fort Worth; p. 63 (B) The Granger
Collection, New York; p. 65 The Thomas Gilcrease Institute of American
History and Art, Tulsa, Oklahoma; p. 67 Peter Newark's American
Pictures; p. 68 The Granger Collection, New York; p. 69 Smithsonian
Institution/Anthropological Collection (photo no. 55,018); p. 70
Popperfoto/UPI; p. 71 Bettmann/Hulton Picture Company; pp. 72–74 The
Granger Collection, New York; p. 76 Picturepoint-London; p. 77 The
Granger Collection, New York; p. 78 (T) Bettmann/Hulton Picture
Company; p. 78 (B) *Cliff Dwellers*, 1913, by George Wesley Bellows,
1882–1925. The Los Angeles County Museum of Art, Los Angeles County
Funds; p. 80 (T) Bettmann/Hulton Picture Company; p. 80 (B) The
Granger Collection, New York; p. 82 *The Strike*, by Robert Koehler. The
Baxandall Company Inc.; pp. 84, 86 Bettmann/Hulton Picture Company;
p. 87 Panama Canal Commission, Miami; p. 88 Trustees of the Imperial
War Museum, London (Detail); p. 89 The New York Public Library; p. 90
The Granger Collection, New York; p. 91 Trustees of the Imperial War
Museum, London; p. 92 The Granger Collection, New York; p. 94 © The
Equitable Life Assurance Society of the United States; p. 95
Bettmann/Hulton Picture Company; p. 96 The Granger Collection, New
York; p. 97 Bettmann/Hulton Picture Company; p. 99 *The Battle Of
Anacostia Flats*, c. 1958. Mort Künstler, collection of Thorne Donnelly, Jr.;
p. 100 The Granger Collection, New York; p. 101 Bettmann/Hulton
Picture Company; p. 102 'Courtesy of Tennessee Valley Authority'; p. 105
National Archives, Washington DC; p. 106 (T) Popperfoto; p. 106 (B)
From *Roosevelt and the United States*, by D.B. O'Callaghan. Published by
Longman, 1966; p. 107 Popperfoto; p. 108 Robert Harding Picture Library;
p. 109 (L) Robert Harding Picture Library; p. 109 (R) Topham Picture
Source; p. 111 © News of the World; p. 113 (T) UPI/Bettmann
Newsphotos; p. 113 (B) Robert Hunt Library; p. 115 (T) UPI/Bettmann
Newsphotos; p. 115 (B) Dominic Photography; p. 117 (T) Camera Press;
p. 117 (B) UPI/Bettmann Newsphotos; p. 118 UPI/Bettmann Newsphotos;
p. 119 UPI/Bettmann Newsphotos; p. 120 Robert Harding Picture Library;
p. 121 Robert Harding Picture Library; p. 122 Camera Press; p. 123
Wayland Publishers Limited; p. 124 The J. Allan Cash Photolibrary; p. 124
(T) The Hutchison Library; p. 125 The Hutchison Library; p. 126
UPI/Bettmann Newsphotos; p. 128 Camera Press; p. 129 (T) Camera Press;
p. 129 (B) Topham Picture Source; p. 130 Topham Picture Source; p. 131
South American Pictures; p. 132 Camera Press; p. 133 UPI/Bettmann
Newsphotos; p. 134 Frank Spooner Pictures; p. 135 UPI/Bettmann
Newsphotos; p. 136 Tony Stone Worldwide; p. 137 (T) Camera Press; p.
137 (B) McDonald's Hamburgers Limited; p. 138 Robert Harding Picture
Library; p. 139 Seagram Building, 1957; Architects: Mies Van der Rohe and
Philip Johnson; Photograph by Ezra Stoller, 1958; Lent by Joseph E
Seagram & Sons Inc.

Cover photographs by: (Top Left) The Granger Collection, New York;
(Top Middle) Anne S.K. Brown Military Collection, Brown University
Library; (Top Right) Rex Features Limited; (Main) The Granger Collection,
New York; (Bottom Left) Robert Harding Picture Library; (Bottom Right)
Peter Newark's American Pictures

Back Cover by: Amon Carter Museum, Fort Worth

Picture Collection by: Sandie Huskinson-Rolfe (PHOTOSEEKERS)

Design by: Sylvia Tate

South America. About 5,000 years later their camp fires were burning on the frozen southern tip of the continent, now called Tierra del Fuego – the Land of Fire.

For many centuries early Amerindians lived as wandering hunters and gatherers of food. Then a more settled way of life began. People living in highland areas of what is now Mexico found a wild grass with tiny seeds that were good to eat. These people became America's first farmers. They cultivated the wild grass with great care to make its seeds larger. Eventually it became Indian corn, or maize. Other cultivated plant foods were developed. By 5000 BC Amerindians in Mexico were growing and eating beans, squash and peppers.

The Pueblo people of present day Arizona and New Mexico were the best organized of the Amerindian farming peoples. They lived in groups of villages, or in towns which were built for safety on the sides and tops of cliffs. They shared terraced buildings made of adobe (mud and straw) bricks, dried in the sun. Some of these buildings contained as many as 800 rooms, crowded together on top of one another. The Pueblo made clothing and blankets from cotton which grew wild in the surrounding deserts. On their feet they wore boot-shaped leather moccasins to protect their legs against the sharp rocks and cactus plants of the desert. For food they grew crops of maize and beans. Irrigation made them successful as farmers. Long before Europeans came to America the Pueblo were building networks of canals across the deserts to bring water to their fields. In one desert valley modern archaeologists have traced canals and ditches which enabled the Pueblo to irrigate 250,000 acres of farmland.

A people called the Apache were the neighbors of the Pueblo. The Apache never became settled farmers. They wandered the deserts and mountains in small bands, hunting deer and gathering wild plants, nuts and roots. They also obtained food by raiding their Pueblo neighbors and stealing it. The Apache were fierce and warlike, and they were much feared by the Pueblo.

The Buffalo Hunt *by Charles M. Russell. Amerindians hunting buffalo.*

The Iroquois were a group of tribes – a "nation" – who lived far away from the Pueblo and the Apache in the thick woods of northeastern North America. Like the Pueblo, the Iroquois were skilled farmers. In fields cleared from the forest they worked together growing beans, squash and twelve different varieties of maize. They were also hunters and fishermen. They used birch bark canoes to carry them swiftly along the rivers and lakes of their forest homeland. The Iroquois lived in permanent villages, in long wooden huts with barrel-shaped roofs. These huts were made from a framework of saplings covered by sheets of elm bark. Each was home to as many as twenty families. Each family had its own apartment on either side of a central hall.

The Iroquois were fierce warriors. They were as feared by their neighbors as the Apache of the western deserts were feared by theirs. Around their huts they built strong wooden stockades to protect their villages from enemies. Eager to win glory for their tribe and fame and honor for themselves, they often fought one another. From boyhood on, male Iroquois were taught to fear neither pain nor death. Bravery in battle was the surest way for a warrior to win respect and a high position in his tribe.

Many miles to the west, on the vast plains of grass that stretched from the Mississippi River to the Rocky Mountains, there was another warrior nation. This group called themselves Dakota, which means "allies." But they were better known by the name which other Amerindians gave to them – Sioux, which means "enemies."

The Sioux grew no crops and built no houses. For food, for shelter and for clothing they depended upon the buffalo. Millions of these large, slow-moving animals wandered across the western grasslands in vast herds. When the buffalo moved, the Sioux moved. The buffalo never remained on one pasture for long, so everything the Sioux owned was designed to be carried easily. Within hours they could take down the tepees, the conical buffalo-skin tents that were their homes, pack their belongings in lightweight leather bags – "parfleches" – and move off after the buffalo. They even carried fire from one camp to the next. A hot ember would be sealed inside a buffalo horn filled with rotted wood. There it would smolder for days, ready to bring warmth from the old village to the new.

The Sioux Creation

In 1933 a Sioux Chief named Luther Standing Bear wrote down some of the ancient legends of his people. This one tells how the Sioux people began:

"Our legends tell us that it was hundreds and perhaps thousands of years ago that the first man sprang from the soil in the great plains. The story says that one morning long ago a lone man awoke, face to the sun, emerging from the soil. Only his head was visible, the rest of his body not yet being shaped. The man looked about, but saw no mountains, no rivers, no forests. There was nothing but soft and quaking mud, for the earth itself was still young. Up and up the man drew himself until he freed his body from the clinging soil. At last he stood upon the earth, but it was not solid, and his first few steps were slow and uncertain. But the sun shone and the man kept his face turned toward it. In time the rays of the sun hardened the face of the earth and strengthened the man and he ran and leaped about, a free and joyous creature. From this man sprang the Dakota nation and, so far as we know, our people have been born and have died upon this plain; and no people have shared it with us until the coming of the European. So this land of the great plains is claimed by the Dakotas as their very own."

To many people the tepee is a symbol of the Amerindian way of life. This large cone-shaped tent was invented by the buffalo hunters of the western grasslands. It was built round a framework of about twelve slim, wooden poles approximately twenty feet long. The thin ends of the poles were tied together with strips of buffalo hide and the poles were raised and spread until their bottom ends formed a circle about fifteen feet in diameter. As many as forty buffalo hides were sewn together then spread over the frame, their ends fastened to the ground by pegs. A doorway covered with a flap of skin was left in the side and an opening at the top acted as a chimney. The outside of the tepee was decorated with painted designs that had religious or historical meanings.

Amerindian tepees.

The lifestyle of the people of North America's northwest coast was different again. They gathered nuts and berries from the forests, but their main food was fish, especially the salmon of the rivers and the ocean. Each spring hundreds of thousands of salmon swam in from the Pacific and fought their way up the fast-flowing rivers to spawn. A few months' work during this season provided the people of the Pacific coast with enough food to last a whole year.

This abundance of food gave the tribes of the Pacific coast time for feasting, for carving and for building. Tribes like the Haida lived in large houses built of wooden planks with elaborately carved gables and doorposts. The most important carvings were on totem poles. These were specially decorated tree trunks which some tribes placed in front of their houses, but which the Haida made part of the house itself. The carvings on the totem pole were a record of the history of the family that lived in the house.

The Amerindian peoples of North America developed widely varied ways of life. All suited the natural environments in which the tribes lived, and they lasted for many centuries. But the arrival of Europeans with their guns, their diseases and their hunger for land would eventually destroy them all.

Potlatches

The "potlatch" was a popular ceremony amongst the wealthy Pacific coast tribes of North America. The word means "gift giving." A modern potlatch is a kind of party at which guests are given gifts, but the original potlatch ceremonies went much further. A chief or head of a family might give away everything that he owned to show how wealthy he was and gain respect. To avoid disgrace, the person receiving the gifts had to give back even more. If he failed to do so his entire family was disgraced.

A Haida potlach.

2

EXPLORERS FROM EUROPE

If you ask "Who discovered America?", the answer that you will usually receive is "Christopher Columbus." But did he? We have seen that the Asian ancestors of the Amerindians arrived in America long before Columbus. Was Columbus the next to arrive?

In the centuries after 1492 stories and legends grew up about other adventurous seamen having reached the New World long before Columbus. One legend tells how a Buddhist monk named Hoei-Shin sailed from China to Mexico in AD 459. Another claims that an Irish monk named Brendan the Bold landed in America in AD 551. Yet another says that the first European to reach the New World was Leif Ericson, "Lucky Leif," a Viking sailor from Iceland. And as recently as 1953 a plaque was set up at Mobile Bay in the modern American state of Alabama which reads "In memory of Prince Madoc, a Welsh explorer who landed on the shores of Mobile Bay in 1170 and left behind, with the Indians, the Welsh language."

All these stories have their supporters. But only in the case of the Vikings have modern scholars found firm evidence to support the old legends. In the 1960s archaeologists uncovered traces of Viking settlements in both Newfoundland and New England.

In Newfoundland the archaeologists found the foundations of huts built in Viking style. They also found iron nails and the weight, or "whorl," from a spindle. These objects were important pieces of evidence that the Vikings had indeed reached

Leif Ericson sighting America. An impression by a nineteenth-century artist.

An Aztec drawing of the Spanish conquest.

America. Until the arrival of Europeans none of the Amerindian tribes knew how to make iron. And the spindle whorl was exactly like those used in known Viking lands such as Iceland.

The Vikings were a sea-going people from Scandinavia in northern Europe. They were proud of their warriors and explorers and told stories called "sagas" about them. The saga of Leif Ericson tells how he sailed from Greenland to the eastern coast of North America in about the year AD 1000. When he found vines with grapes on them growing there, he named the place where he landed "Vinland the Good."

Other Vikings followed Leif to Vinland. But the settlements they made there did not last. The hostility of the local Amerindians and the dangers of the northern seas combined to make them give up their attempt to colonize Vinland. The Vikings sailed away and their discovery of Vinland was forgotten except by their storytellers.

It was the Spanish who began the lasting European occupation of America. When Columbus returned to Spain he took back with him some jewelry that he had obtained in America. This jewelry was important because it was made of gold. In the next fifty years thousands of treasure-hungry Spanish

Why is America called "America"

Why did European geographers give the name America to the lands that Columbus discovered? Why did they not name them instead after Columbus?

The reason is that to the end of his life Columbus believed that his discoveries were part of Asia. The man who did most to correct this mistaken idea was Amerigo Vespucci. Vespucci was an Italian sailor from the city of Florence. During the late 1490s he wrote some letters in which he described two voyages of exploration that he had made along the coasts of South America. He was sure, he wrote, that these coasts were part of a new continent.

Some years later Vespucci's letters were read by a German scholar who was revising an old geography of the world. The letters convinced the scholar that Vespucci was correct, and that the lands beyond the Atlantic were a new continent. To honor Vespucci the scholar named them America, using the feminine form of Vespucci's first name as the other continents had female names.

9

The Fountain of Youth

To sixteenth century Europeans America was a land of marvels, a place where nothing was impossible. Some even believed that there they might discover a way to regain their lost youth.

Ponce de León was a Spanish conquistador who came to the New World with Columbus on the explorer's second voyage. He became the governor of the Caribbean island of Puerto Rico. The Amerindian people of Puerto Rico told de León that to the north lay a land rich in gold. This northern land, they said, also had an even more precious treasure – a fountain whose waters gave everlasting youth to all those who drank from it. In the spring of 1513 de León set off in search of the magic fountain. He landed in present day Florida and sailed all round its coast searching for the miraculous waters.

Ponce de León never found the Fountain of Youth. But he did claim Florida for Spain. In 1565 Spanish settlers founded St. Augustine there, the first permanent European settlement on the mainland of North America.

adventurers crossed the Atlantic Ocean to search for more of the precious metal. It was a lust for gold that led Hernán Cortés to conquer the Aztecs in the 1520s. The Aztecs were a wealthy, city-building Amerindian people who lived in what is today Mexico. In the 1530s the same lust for gold caused Francisco Pizarro to attack the equally wealthy empire of the Incas of Peru. A stream of looted treasure began to flow across the Atlantic to Spain from a new empire built up by such conquerors – "conquistadores" – in Central and South America.

In the years that followed, other Spanish conquistadores took the search for gold to North America. Between 1539 and 1543 Hernando de Soto and Francisco Coronado, working separately, explored much of the southern part of what is now the United States. De Soto landed in Florida from Cuba. He led his expedition westward, discovering the Mississippi River and traveling beyond it into Texas and Oklahoma. Coronado traveled north from Mexico, searching for the "Seven Cities of Gold" that Amerindian legends said lay hidden somewhere in the desert. He never found them. But he and his men became the first Europeans to see the Grand Canyon of the Colorado River and they journeyed as far east as Kansas before returning to Mexico.

Discovery of the Mississippi, *a romanticized nineteenth-century painting by William H Powell. De Soto and his followers are shown displaying their cannon and a cross to a group of frightened Amerindians.*

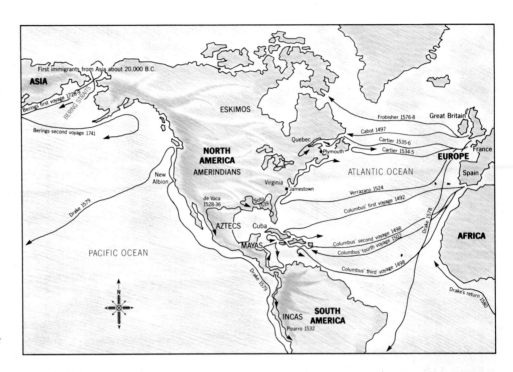

The exploration and settlement of America.

The journeys of men such as de Soto and Coronado gave Spain a claim to a large amount of land in North America. They also led to the founding of some of the earliest permanent European settlements there. In 1565 Spanish settlers founded St. Augustine on the coast of present-day Florida. In 1609 other settlers founded Santa Fe in New Mexico.

The growing wealth of Spain made other European nations envious. They became eager to share the riches of the New World. In 1497 King Henry VII of England hired an Italian seaman named John Cabot to explore the new lands and to look again for a passage to Asia. Cabot sailed far to the north of the route Columbus had followed. Eventually he reached the rocky coast of Newfoundland. At first Cabot thought that this was China. A year later he made a second westward crossing of the Atlantic. This time he sailed south along the coast of North America as far as Chesapeake Bay.

Cabot found no gold and no passage to the East. But his voyages were valuable for the English. In later years English governments used them to support their claims to own most of the east coast of North America.

The French also sent explorers to North America. In 1524 the French king, Francis I, sent an Italian sailor named Giovanni Verrazano for the same purpose as Columbus and Cabot – to find lands rich in gold and a new sea route to Asia. Verrazano sailed the full length of the east coast of America, but found neither. However, he anchored his ship in what is now the harbor of New York. Today a bridge which carries his name, the Verrazano Narrows Bridge, is one of the city's most impressive sights.

Ten years later another French explorer, a fisherman from Normandy named Jacques Cartier, discovered the St. Lawrence River. He returned to France and reported that the forests lining the river's shores were full of fur-bearing animals and that its waters were full of fish. The next year he sailed further up the river, reaching the site of the present-day city of Montreal. Cartier failed to find the way to Asia that he was looking for, but he gave France a claim to what would later become Canada.

Claiming that you owned land in the New World was one thing. Actually making it yours was something quite different. Europeans could only do this by establishing settlements of their own people. By the seventeenth century plenty of people in Europe were ready to settle in America. Some hoped to become rich by doing so. Others hoped to find safety from religious or political persecution. In the hundred years after 1600, Europeans set up many colonies in North America for reasons like these.

3
VIRGINIAN BEGINNINGS

Replicas of the ships that carried the first settlers to Jamestown in 1617.

All through the night the storm blew the three small ships northwards. For hours the frightened sailors struggled with wet ropes and snapping canvas sails. At last, as dawn colored the eastern skies, the storm came to an end. Men dropped to the decks, exhausted. Some fell asleep. Excited shouts awoke them. "Land! Land!" The sailors rushed to the sides of the ships. There, at last, was the land for which they had been searching – Virginia. It was the morning of April 26 in the year 1607.

A few weeks later, on May 20, the sailors tied their ships to trees on the banks of a broad and deep river. They named the river the James, in honor of James I, king of England, the country from which they had set sail five long months before. Just over a hundred men went ashore. On the swampy banks they began cutting down bushes and trees and building rough shelters for themselves. By the end of the year two out of every three of them were dead. But their little group of huts became the first lasting English settlement in America. They named it Jamestown.

The early years of the Jamestown settlement were hard ones. This was partly the fault of the settlers themselves. The site they had chosen was low-lying and malarial. And although their English homeland was many miles away across a dangerous ocean, they failed to grow enough food to feed themselves. They were too busy dreaming of gold.

The settlers had been sent to Jamestown by a group of rich London investors. These investors had formed the Virginia Company. The Company's purpose was to set up colonies along the Atlantic coast of North America, between 34° and 38° north latitude. It was a joint stock company – that is, the investors paid the costs of its expeditions and in return were given the right to divide up any profits it made. The Jamestown settlers were employees of the Virginia Company. The Company's directors hoped that the settlers would find pearls, silver, or some other valuable product in Virginia and so bring them a quick profit on their investment. Most of all, they hoped that the colonists would find gold, as the Spanish conquistadores had done in Mexico.

The colonists eagerly obeyed the Company's orders to search for gold. By doing so they hoped to become rich themselves. There was "no talk, no hope nor work, but dig gold, wash gold, load gold", wrote one of their leaders, Captain John Smith.

And then the colonists began to die – in ones, in twos, finally in dozens. Some died in Amerindian attacks, some of diseases, some of starvation. By April 1608, out of a total of 197 Englishmen who had landed in Virginia only fifty-three were still alive. "Our men were destroyed by cruel diseases," wrote a colonist who survived, "swellings, fluxes, burning fevers and by wars. But most died of famine. There were never Englishmen left in a foreign country in such misery as we were in Virginia."

Jamestown reached its lowest point in the winter of 1609–1610. Of the 500 colonists living in the settlement in October 1609, only sixty were still alive in March 1610. This was "the starving time." Stories reached England about settlers who were so desperate for food that they dug up and ate the body of an Amerindian they had killed during an attack.

Yet new settlers continued to arrive. The Virginia Company gathered homeless children from the streets of London and sent them out to the colony. Then it sent a hundred convicts from London's prisons. Such emigrants were often unwilling to go. The Spanish ambassador in London told of three condemned criminals who were given the choice of being hanged or sent to Virginia. Two agreed to go, but the third chose to hang.

Some Virginia emigrants sailed willingly, however. For many English people these early years of the seventeenth century were a time of hunger and suffering. Incomes were low, but the prices of food and clothing climbed higher every year. Many people were without work. And if the crops failed, they starved. Some English people decided that it was worth risking the possibility of hardships in Virginia to escape from the certainty of them at home. For Virginia had one great attraction that England lacked: plentiful land. This seemed more important than the reports of disease, starvation and cannibalism there. In England, as in Europe generally, the land was owned by the rich. In Virginia a poor man could hope for a farm of his own to feed his family.

The captain and the princess

Captain John Smith was the most able of the original Jamestown settlers. An energetic 27-year-old soldier and explorer, he had already had a life full of action when he landed there in 1607. It was he who organized the first Jamestown colonists and forced them to work. If he had not done that, the infant settlement would probably have collapsed.

When food supplies ran out Smith set off into the forests to buy corn from the Amerindians. On one of these expeditions he was taken prisoner. According to a story that he told later (which not everyone believed), the Amerindians were going to beat his brains out when Pocahontas, the twelve-year-old daughter of the chief, Powhatan, saved his life by shielding his body with her own. Pocahontas went on to play an important part in Virginia's survival, bringing food to the starving settlers. "She, next under God," wrote Smith, "was the instrument to preserve this colony from death, famine and utter confusion."

In 1609 Smith was badly injured in a gunpowder explosion and was sent back to England. Five years later, in 1614, Pocahontas married the tobacco planter John Rolfe. In 1616 she travelled to England with him and was presented at court to King James I. It was there that the portrait you see here was painted. Pocahontas died of smallpox in 1617 while waiting to board a ship to carry her back to Virginia with her newborn son. When the son grew up he returned to Virginia. Many Virginians today claim to be descended from him and so from Pocahontas.

A portrait of Pocahontas, painted during her visit to London.

Brides for sale

Very few women settled in early Virginia, so in 1619 the Virginia Company shipped over a group of ninety young women as wives for its settlers. To obtain a bride the would-be husbands had to pay the Company "120 pounds weight of best tobacco leaf." The price must have seemed reasonable, for within a very short time all the young women were married.

A label from Wills tobacco. Wills was one of the most famous English tobacco companies.

For a number of years after 1611, military governors ran Virginia like a prison camp. They enforced strict rules to make sure that work was done. But it was not discipline that saved Virginia. It was a plant that grew like a weed there: tobacco. Earlier visitors to America, like Sir Walter Raleigh, had brought the first dried leaves of tobacco to England. Its popularity had been growing ever since, for smoking, for taking as snuff, even for brewing into a drink. In Virginia a young settler named John Rolfe discovered how to dry, or "cure," the leaves in a new way, to make them milder. In 1613 Rolfe shipped the first load of Virginia tobacco to England. London merchants paid high prices because of its high quality.

Soon most of the Virginia settlers were busy growing tobacco. They cleared new land along the rivers and ploughed up the streets of Jamestown itself to plant more. They even used it as money. The price of a good horse in Virginia, for example, was sixteen pounds of top quality tobacco. The possibility of becoming rich by growing tobacco brought wealthy

men to Virginia. They obtained large stretches of land and brought workers from England to clear trees and plant tobacco. Soon the houses and barns of their estates, or "plantations," could be seen through the trees along the banks of the James river.

Most of the workers on these early plantations were "indentured servants" from England. They promised to work for an employer for an agreed number of years – about seven was average – in exchange for food and clothes. At the end they became free to work for themselves. Luckier ones were given a small piece of land to start a farm of their own – if they were still alive. Life in Virginia

Martin's Hundred, an early English settlement on the James river. A modern artist's impression, based on archaeological evidence.

continued to be hard. "I have eaten more in a day at home than I have here for a week," wrote a young man named Richard Frethorne in a letter to his parents back in England.

The same was true for many in Virginia. Nor was hunger the only problem. Diseases like malaria and wars against the Amerindians continued to kill hundreds of settlers. Between 1619 and 1621 about 3,560 people left England to settle in Virginia. Before those years were over, 3,000 of them were dead.

But the survivors stayed. In 1619 there was an important change in the way they were governed.

Virginia's affairs had been controlled so far by governors sent over by the Virginia Company. Now the Company allowed a body called the House of Burgesses to be set up. The burgesses were elected representatives from the various small settlements along Virginia's rivers. They met to advise the governor on the laws the colony needed. Though few realized it at the time, the Virginia House of Burgesses was the start of an important tradition in American life – that people should have a say in decisions about matters that concern them.

The House of Burgesses met for the first time in August 1619. In that same month Virginia saw another important beginning. A small Dutch warship anchored at Jamestown. On board were twenty captured black Africans. The ship's captain sold them to the settlers as indentured servants.

The blacks were set to work in the tobacco fields with white indentured servants from England. But there was a very serious difference between their position and that of the whites working beside them. White servants were indentured for a fixed number of years. Their masters might treat them badly, but they knew that one day they would be free. Black servants had no such hope. Their indenture was for life. In fact they were slaves – although it was years before their masters openly admitted the fact.

The Virginia Company never made a profit. By 1624 it had run out of money. The English government put an end to the Company and made itself responsible for the Virginia colonists. There were still very few of them. Fierce Amerindian attacks in 1622 had destroyed several settlements and killed over 350 colonists. Out of nearly 10,000 settlers sent out since 1607, a 1624 census showed only 1,275 survivors.

But their hardships had toughened the survivors. Building a new homeland in the steamy river valleys of Virginia had proved harder and taken longer than anyone had expected. But this first society of English people overseas had put down living roots into the American soil. Other struggles lay ahead, but by 1624 one thing was clear – Virginia would survive.

The lost colony

The Jamestown settlers were not the first English people to visit Virginia. Twenty years earlier the adventurer Sir Walter Raleigh had sent ships to find land in the New World where English people might settle. He named the land they visited Virginia, in honor of Elizabeth, England's un-married Queen.

In July 1585, 108 English settlers landed on Roanoke Island, off the coast of what is now the state of North Carolina. They built houses and a fort, planted crops and searched – without success – for gold. But they ran out of food and made enemies of the local Amerindian inhabitants. In less than a year they gave up and sailed back to England.

In 1587 Raleigh tried again. His ships landed 118 settlers on Roanoke, including fourteen family groups. The colonists were led by an artist and mapmaker named John White, who had been a member of the 1585 expedition. Among them were White's daughter and her husband. On August 18th the couple became the parents of Virginia Dare, the first English child to be born in America.

In August White returned to England for supplies. Three years passed before he was able to return. When his ships reached Roanoke in August 1590, he found the settlement deserted. There was no sign of what had happened to its people except a word carved on a tree – "Croaton," the home of a friendly Indian chief, fifty miles to the south. Some believe that the Roanoke settlers were carried off by Spanish soldiers from Florida. Others think that they may have decided to go to live with friendly Indians on the mainland. They were never seen, or heard of, again.

4

PURITAN NEW ENGLAND

"Pilgrims" are people who make a journey for religious reasons. But for Americans the word has a special meaning. To them it means a small group of English men and women who sailed across the Atlantic Ocean in the year 1620. The group's members came to be called the Pilgrims because they went to America to find religious freedom. Sometimes Americans call them the Pilgrim Fathers. This is because they see them as the most important of the founders of the future United States of America.

The Europe that the Pilgrims left behind them was torn by religious quarrels. For more than a thousand years Roman Catholic Christianity had been the religion of most of its people. By the sixteenth century, however, some Europeans had begun to doubt the teachings of the Catholic Church. They were also growing angry at the wealth and worldly pride of its leaders.

Early in the century a German monk named Martin Luther quarreled with these leaders. He claimed that individual human beings did not need the Pope or the priests of the Catholic Church to enable them to speak to God. A few years later a French lawyer named John Calvin put forward similar ideas. Calvin claimed that each individual was directly and personally responsible to God. Because they protested against the teachings and customs of the Catholic Church, religious reformers like Luther and Calvin were called "Protestants." Their ideas spread quickly through northern Europe.

Few people believed in religious toleration at this time. In most countries people were expected to have the same religion as their ruler. This was the case in England. In the 1530s the English king, Henry VIII, formed a national church with himself as its head. In the later years of the sixteenth century many English people believed that this Church of England was still too much like the Catholic Church. They disliked the power of its bishops. They disliked its elaborate ceremonies and the rich decorations of its churches. They also questioned many of its teachings. Such people wanted the Church of England to become

more plain and simple, or "pure." Because of this they were called Puritans. The ideas of John Calvin appealed particularly strongly to them.

When James I became King of England in 1603 he warned the Puritans that he would drive them from the land if they did not accept his ideas on religion. His bishops began fining the Puritans and putting them in prison. To escape this persecution, a small group of them left England and went to Holland. Holland was the only country in Europe whose government allowed religious freedom at this time.

The people of Holland welcomed the little group of exiles. But the Puritans never felt at home there. After much thought and much prayer they decided to move again. Some of them – the Pilgrims – decided to go to America.

First they returned briefly to England. Here they persuaded the Virginia Company to allow them to settle in the northern part of its American lands. On September 16, 1620, the Pilgrims left the English

The Mayflower Compact

When the Pilgrims arrived off the coast of America they faced many dangers and difficulties. They did not want to put themselves in further danger by quarreling with one another. Before landing at Plymouth, therefore, they wrote out an agreement. In this document they agreed to work together for the good of all. The agreement was signed by all forty-one men on board the *Mayflower*. It became known as the Mayflower Compact. In the Compact the Plymouth settlers agreed to set up a government – a "civil body politic" – to make "just and equal laws" for their new settlement. All of them, Pilgrims and Strangers alike, promised that they would obey these laws. In the difficult years which followed, the Mayflower Compact served the colonists well. It is remembered today as one of the first important documents in the history of democratic government in America.

The Pilgrim Fathers landing in America.

port of Plymouth and headed for America. They were accompanied by a number of other emigrants they called "Strangers."

The Pilgrims' ship was an old trading vessel, the *Mayflower*. For years the *Mayflower* had carried wine across the narrow seas between France and England. Now it faced a much more dangerous voyage. For sixty-five days the *Mayflower* battled through the rolling waves of the north Atlantic Ocean. At last, on November 9, 1620, it reached Cape Cod, a sandy hook of land in what is now the state of Massachusetts.

Cape Cod is far to the north of the land granted to the Pilgrims by the Virginia Company. But the Pilgrims did not have enough food and water, and many were sick. They decided to land at the best place they could find. On December 21, 1620, they rowed ashore and set up camp at a place they named Plymouth.

"The season it was winter," wrote one of their leaders, "and those who know the winters of that country know them to be sharp and violent with cruel and fierce storms." The Pilgrims' chances of surviving were not high. The frozen ground and the deep snow made it difficult for them to build houses. They had very little food. Before spring came, half of the little group of a hundred settlers were dead.

But the Pilgrims were determined to succeed. The fifty survivors built better houses. They learned how to fish and hunt. Friendly Amerindians gave them seed corn and showed them how to plant it. It was not the end of their hardships, but when a ship arrived in Plymouth in 1622 and offered to take passengers back to England, not one of the Pilgrims accepted.

Other English Puritans followed the Pilgrims to America. Ten years later a much larger group of almost a thousand colonists settled nearby in what became the Boston area. These people left England to escape the rule of a new king, Charles I. Charles was even less tolerant than his father James had been of people who disagreed with his policies in religion and government.

The Boston settlement prospered from the start. Its population grew quickly as more and more Puritans left England to escape persecution. Many years later, in 1691, it combined with the Plymouth colony under the name of Massachusetts.

The ideas of the Massachusetts Puritans had a lasting influence on American society. One of their first leaders, John Winthrop, said that they should build an ideal community for the rest of mankind to learn from. "We shall be like a city on a hill," said

17

Winthrop. "The eyes of all people are upon us." To this day many Americans continue to see their country in this way, as a model for other nations to copy.

The Puritans of Massachusetts believed that governments had a duty to make people obey God's will. They passed laws to force people to attend church and laws to punish drunks and adulterers. Even men who let their hair grow long could be in trouble.

Roger Williams, a Puritan minister in a settlement called Salem, believed that it was wrong to run the affairs of Massachusetts in this way. He objected particularly to the fact that the same men controlled both the church and the government. Williams believed that church and state should be separate and that neither should interfere with the other.

Williams' repeated criticisms made the Massachusetts leaders angry. In 1535 they sent men to arrest him. But Williams escaped and went south, where he was joined by other discontented people from Massachusetts. On the shores of Narragansett Bay Williams and his followers set up a new colony called Rhode Island. Rhode Island promised its citizens complete religious freedom and separation of church and state. To this day these ideas are still very important to Americans.

The leaders of Massachusetts could not forgive the people of Rhode Island for thinking so differently from themselves. They called the breakaway colony "the land of the opposite-minded."

Plymouth Puritans going to church.

William Penn signing a treaty with the Amerindians.

By the end of the seventeenth century a string of English colonies stretched along the east coast of North America. More or less in the middle was Pennsylvania. This was founded in 1681 by William Penn. Under a charter from the English king, Charles II, Penn was the proprietor, or owner, of Pennsylvania.

Penn belonged to a religious group, the Society of Friends, commonly called Quakers. Quakers refused to swear oaths or to take part in wars. These customs had helped to make them very unpopular with English governments. When Penn promised his fellow Quakers that in Pennsylvania they would be free to follow their own ways, many of them emigrated there.

Penn's promise of religious freedom, together with his reputation for dealing fairly with people, brought settlers from other European countries to Pennsylvania. From Ireland came settlers who made new farms in the western forests of the colony. Many Germans came also. Most were members of small religious groups who had left Germany to escape persecution. They were known as the Pennsylvania Dutch. This was because English people at this time called most north Europeans "Dutch."

New York had previously been called New Amsterdam. It had first been settled in 1626. In 1664 the English captured it from the Dutch and re-named it New York. A few years later, in 1670, the English founded the new colonies of North and South Carolina. The last English colony to be founded in North America was Georgia, settled in 1733.

America →
canonic
Protestant
puritans
pilgrims
Quakers

4 PURITAN NEW ENGLAND

Thanksgiving

Every year on the fourth Thursday in November Americans celebrate a holiday called Thanksgiving. The first people to celebrate this day were the Pilgrims. In November, 1621, they sat down to eat together and to give thanks to God for enabling them to survive the hardships of their first year in America.

The Pilgrims were joined at their feast by local Amerindians. The Wampanoag and Pequamid people of the nearby forests had shared corn with the Pilgrims and shown them the best places to catch fish. Later the Amerindians had given seed corn to the English settlers and shown them how to plant crops that would grow well in the American soil. Without them there would have been no Thanksgiving.

The first Thanksgiving.

Minuit buys Manhattan

In the 1620s settlers from Holland founded a colony they called New Netherlands along the banks of the Hudson River. At the mouth of the Hudson lies Manhattan Island, the present site of New York City. An Amerindian people called the Shinnecock used the island for hunting and fishing, although they did not live on it.

In 1626 Peter Minuit, the first Dutch governor of the New Netherlands, "bought" Manhattan from the Shinnecock. He paid them about twenty-four dollars' worth of cloth, beads and other trade goods. Like all Amerindians, the Shinnecock believed that land belonged to all men. They thought that what they were selling to the Dutch was the right to share Manhattan with themselves. But the Dutch, like other Europeans, believed that buying land made it theirs alone.

These different beliefs about land ownership were to be a major cause of conflict between Europeans and Amerindians for many years to come. And the bargain price that Peter Minuit paid for Manhattan Island became part of American folklore.

5

COLONIAL LIFE IN AMERICA

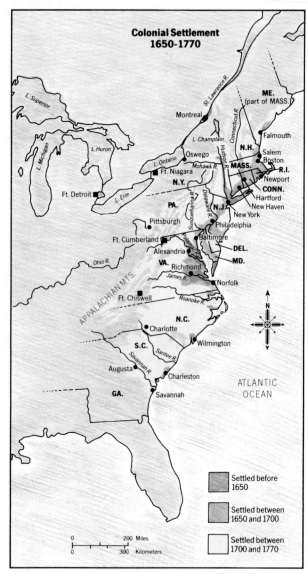

Colonial Settlement 1650-1770

Settled before 1650

Settled between 1650 and 1700

Settled between 1700 and 1770

The settlement of eastern North America by the English.

By the year 1733 the English owned thirteen separate colonies along the Atlantic coast of North America. The colonies stretched from New Hampshire in the north to Georgia in the south. Most people divided them into three main groups. Each group had its own way of life and character.

In the far north was the New England group, centered on Massachusetts. Since the time of the Pilgrims the people of New England had spread inland and along the coast. Most were small farmers or craftsmen, working the stony soil and governing themselves in small towns and villages.

Other New Englanders depended on the sea for a living. They felled the trees of the region's forests to build ships. In these they sailed to catch cod or to trade with England and the West Indies. Boston and other coastal towns grew into busy ports. Their prosperity depended on trade.

The nearest colonies to the south of New England were called the Middle Colonies. The biggest were New York and Pennsylvania. As in New England, most of their people lived by farming. But in the cities of New York and Philadelphia there were growing numbers of craftsmen and merchants. Philadelphia was the capital of Pennsylvania. By 1770 it was the largest city in America, with 28,000 inhabitants.

Philadelphia in 1720, a contemporary painting by Peter Cooper.

Abbreviations:

ME.	Maine	**N.J.**	New Jersey
N.H.	New Hampshire	**DEL.**	Delaware
MASS.	Massachusetts	**MD.**	Maryland
R.I.	Rhode Island	**VA.**	Virginia
N.Y.	New York	**N.C.**	North Carolina
CONN.	Connecticut	**S.C.**	South Carolina
PA.	Pennsylvania	**GA.**	Georgia

Cities and trade

In 1760 most Americans were farmers. But important towns had grown up whose people earned their living by trade and manufacturing. Philadelphia, with its 28,000 inhabitants, was the largest. An English visitor marveled at the speed with which it had grown. "It is not an hundred years since the first tree was cut where the city now stands," he wrote, "and now it has more than three thousand six hundred houses."

The size of Philadelphia was not the only thing that impressed visitors. Long before most English cities, its streets were paved with brick and street lamps were lit every night. The only exception to this was when the moon was shining, for the citizens of Philadelphia did not believe in wasting money!

The next biggest cities after Philadelphia were New York and Boston, with about 25,000 people each. All three towns owed much of their prosperity to the profits of the transatlantic trade that they carried on with England. Their ships exported furs, timber, tobacco, and cotton, and brought back fashionable clothes, fine furniture, and other manufactured goods. Their merchants also traded with one another.

This inter-American trade helped to produce a feeling between the cities that they all belonged to the same American nation.

The people of the Middle Colonies were usually more tolerant of religious and other differences than the New Englanders. Many of them also had German, Dutch or Swedish ancestors rather than English ones.

The Southern Colonies of Virginia, the Carolinas and Georgia formed the third group. In their hot and fertile river valleys wealthy landowners farmed large plantations. They lived in fine houses, with wide, cool verandahs from which they could look out over their fields of tobacco or cotton. Most of the work in the fields was done by black slaves. Slavery was rare in the other American colonies. But the prosperity of the plantation-owning southerners was already beginning to depend upon it.

The houses of the southern plantation owners had expensive furniture, much of it imported from Europe. Close by stood groups of smaller, more simple buildings – stables, washhouses, blacksmiths' shops and the little huts in which the black slaves lived. And almost always a river flowed nearby, with a wharf where sea-going ships could be loaded to carry the plantation's crops to England.

In all three groups of colonies most people still lived less than fifty miles from the coast. This was called "the tidewater" period of settlement. Those people furthest inland had traveled up tidal rivers like the James and the Hudson, clearing the trees and setting up farms along their banks.

During the fifty years after 1733 settlers moved deeper into the continent. They traveled west into

central Pennsylvania, cutting down forests of oak trees to make hilly farms. They spread westward along the river valleys in Virginia, the Carolinas and Georgia. They moved north along the fertile valley of the Mohawk River of New York.

Making a new settlement always began in the same way. The settlers cleared the land of trees, then cut the trees into logs and planks. They used these to build a house and a barn. They then ploughed between the tree stumps, sowed their seeds, and four months later harvested the crops of corn and wheat. If their soil was fertile the settlers lived well. But if the soil was rocky, or poor in plant foods, life could be hard and disappointing. Settlers with poor soil often left their farms and moved westward, to try again on more fertile land. As they traveled inland they passed fewer and fewer farms and villages. At last there were none at all. This area, where European settlement came to an end and the forest homelands of the Amerindians began, was called the frontier.

Fresh waves of settlers pushed the frontier steadily westwards in their search for fertile soil. They would often pass by land that seemed unsuitable for farming. Because of this, frontier farms and villages were often separated by miles of unsettled land. A family might be a day's journey from its nearest neighbors. For such reasons the people of frontier communities had to rely upon themselves for almost everything they needed. They grew their own food and built their own houses. They made the clothing they wore and the tools they used. They developed their own kinds of music, entertainment, art and forms of religious worship.

A special spirit, or attitude, grew out of this frontier way of life. People needed to be tough, independent and self-reliant. Yet they also needed to work together, helping each other with such tasks as clearing land and building houses and barns. The combination of these two ideas – a strong belief that individuals had to help themselves and a need for them to cooperate with one another – strengthened the feeling that people were equal and that nobody should have special rights and privileges.

The frontier way of life helped democratic ideas to flourish in America. Today's Americans like to think that many of the best values and attitudes of the modern United States can be traced back to the frontier experiences of their pioneer ancestors.

Daniel Boone and the Wilderness Road

In the 1760s land-hungry American settlers moving westwards were stopped by a major obstacle, the Appalachian Mountains. This thickly forested mountain range runs roughly parallel to the Atlantic coast of North America and stretches for hundreds of miles.

When settlers reached the foothills of the Appalachians they found waterfalls and rapids blocking the rivers they had been following westwards. In 1775 a hunter and explorer named Daniel Boone led a party of settlers into the mountains. Boone is said to have claimed that he had been "ordained by God to settle the wilderness." With a party of thirty axmen he cut a track called the Wilderness Road through the forested Cumberland Gap, a natural pass in the Appalachians.

Beyond the Cumberland Gap lay rich, rolling grasslands. In the years which followed, Boone's Wilderness Road enabled thousands of settlers to move with horses, wagons, and cattle into these fertile lands. They now make up the American states of Kentucky and Tennessee.

Daniel Boone escorting settlers on the Wilderness Road.

A plantation port in Chesapeake Bay.

Governors and assemblies

All the English colonies in America shared a tradition of representative government. This means that in all of them people had a say in how they were governed. Each colony had its own government. At the head of this government was a governor, chosen in most cases by the English king. To rule effectively, these governors depended upon the cooperation of assemblies elected by the colonists.

In most of the colonies all white males who owned some land had the right to vote. Since so many colonists owned land, this meant that far more people had the vote in America than in England itself – or in any other European country at this time.

THE ROOTS OF REVOLUTION

In the eighteenth century Britain and France fought several major wars. The struggle between them went on in Europe, Asia and North America.

In North America, France claimed to own Canada and Louisiana. Canada, or New France, extended north from the St. Lawrence River and south towards the frontier areas of the English colonies on the Atlantic coast. Louisiana, named for the French king, Louis XIV, stretched across the center of the continent. It included all the lands drained by the Mississippi River and its tributaries.

In the middle of the eighteenth century most of the forests and plains of both of these vast areas were still unexplored by Europeans. The French claim to own them was based upon journeys made in the previous century by two famous explorers.

The first of these explorers was Samuel de Champlain. From 1603 onwards, Champlain explored the lands on both sides of the St. Lawrence River and set up trading posts there. The two most important of these posts later grew into the cities of Quebec and Montreal.

The other French explorer was René La Salle. La Salle was a fur trader, explorer and empire builder all in one. In the 1670s he explored the valley of the Mississippi. "It is nearly all so beautiful and so fertile," he wrote. "So full of meadows, brooks and rivers; so abounding in fish and venison that one can find here all that is needed to support flourishing colonies. The soil will produce everything that is grown in France."

The British attack on Quebec.

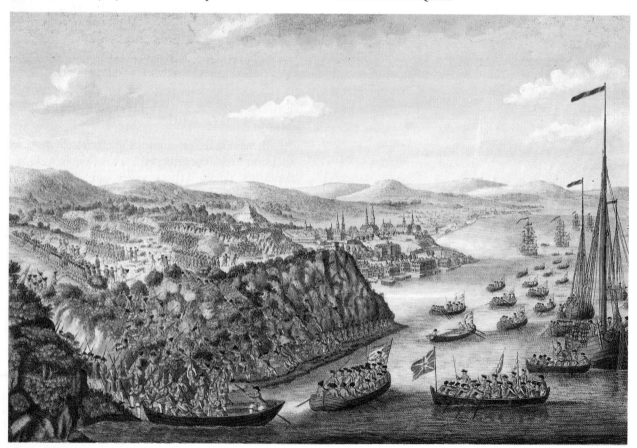

La Salle paddled for thousands of miles down the Mississippi. At last he reached the Gulf of Mexico, where the great river empties into the sea. Some years later the French set up a trading post there. In future years this became the city of New Orleans.

The French claim that Louisiana belonged to them worried both the British government and the American colonists. A glance at a map explains why. Suppose France sent soldiers to occupy the Mississippi valley. They would be able to keep the colonists to the east of the Appalachian Mountains and stop them from moving westwards.

After several wars earlier in the eighteenth century, in 1756 Britain and France began fighting the Seven Years War. This is known to Americans as the French and Indian War.

Led by their forceful Prime Minister, William Pitt the Elder, the British sent money and soldiers to North America. In 1758 British and colonial forces captured the French strongholds of Louisburg on the Gulf of St. Lawrence and Fort Duquesne on the Ohio River. In 1759 they took Quebec. In 1760 Montreal fell to them. The war was ended by the Peace of Paris, which was signed in 1763. France gave up its claim to Canada and to all of North America east of the Mississippi River.

Britain had won an Empire. But its victory led directly to conflict with its American colonies. Even before the final defeat of the French, colonists in search of better land began to move over the Appalachian Mountains into the Ohio valley. To prevent war with the Amerindian tribes who lived in the area, the English king, George III, issued a proclamation in 1763. It forbade colonists to settle west of the Appalachians until proper treaties had been made with the Amerindians.

The king's proclamation angered the colonists. They became angrier still when the British government told them that they must pay new taxes on imports of sugar, coffee, textiles, and other goods. The government also told them that they must feed and find shelter for British soldiers it planned to keep in the colonies. These orders seemed perfectly fair to British politicians. It had cost British taxpayers a lot of money to defend the colonies during the French and Indian War. Surely, they reasoned, the colonists could not object to repaying some of this money?

Trade laws and "sleeping dogs"

Until the 1760s most Americans seemed quite content to be ruled by Britain. An important reason for this was the presence of the French in North America. So long as France held Canada and Louisiana, the colonists felt that they needed the British navy and soldiers to protect them.

Another reason the colonists accepted British rule was that the British government rarely interfered in colonial affairs.

A century earlier the British Parliament had passed some laws called Navigation Acts. These listed certain products called "enumerated commodities" that the colonies were forbidden to export to any country except England. It was easy for the colonists to avoid obeying these laws. The long American coastline made smuggling easy.

The colonists did not care much either about import taxes, or duties, that they were supposed to pay on goods from abroad. The duties were light and carelessly collected. Few merchants bothered to pay them. And again, smuggling was easy. Ships could unload their cargoes on hundreds of lonely wharves without customs officers knowing.

When a British Prime Minister named Robert Walpole was asked why he did not do more to enforce the trade laws, he replied: "Let sleeping dogs lie." He knew the independent spirit of the British colonists in America and wanted no trouble with them. The trouble began when later British politicians forgot his advice and awoke the "sleeping dogs."

But the colonists did object. Merchants believed that the new import taxes would make it more difficult for them to trade at a profit. Other colonists believed that the taxes would raise their costs of living. They also feared that if British troops stayed in America they might be used to force them to obey the British government. This last objection was an early example of a belief that became an important tradition in American political life – that people should not allow governments to become too powerful.

A cartoon showing the burial of the Stamp Act.

In 1765 the British Parliament passed another new law called the Stamp Act. This too was intended to raise money to pay for the defense of the colonies. It said that the colonists had to buy special tax stamps and attach them to newspapers, licenses, and legal papers such as wills and mortgages.

Ever since the early years of the Virginia settlement Americans had claimed the right to elect representatives to decide the taxes they paid. Now they insisted that as "freeborn Englishmen" they could be taxed only by their own colonial assemblies. We have no representatives in the British Parliament, they said, so what right does it have to tax us? "No taxation without representation" became their demand.

In 1765 representatives from nine colonies met in New York. They formed the "Stamp Act Congress" and organized opposition to the Stamp Act. All over the colonies merchants and shopkeepers refused to sell British goods until the Act was withdrawn. In Boston and other cities angry mobs attacked government officials selling the stamps. Most colonists simply refused to use them.

The Boston Tea Party.

Samuel Adams and the Boston Massacre

Samuel Adams was a politician and writer who organized opposition in Massachusetts to the British tax laws. He believed in the idea of "no taxation without representation." In articles and speeches he attacked the British government's claim that it had the right to tax the colonists.

On March 5, 1770, a Boston mob began to shout insults at a group of British soldiers. Angry words were exchanged. Sticks and stones began to fly through the air at the soldiers. One of the crowd tried to take a soldier's gun and the soldier shot him. Without any order from the officer in charge, more shots were fired and three more members of the crowd fell dead. Several others were wounded.

Samuel Adams used this "Boston Massacre" to stir up American opinion against the British. He wrote a letter which inaccurately described the happening as an unprovoked attack on a peaceful group of citizens. He sent out copies of the letter to all the colonies. To make his account more

Paul Revere's engraving of the Boston Massacre.

convincing, he asked a Boston silversmith named Paul Revere to make a dramatic picture of the "Massacre." Hundreds of copies were printed.

Adams' letter and Revere's picture were seen by thousands of people throughout the colonies. Together they did a great deal to strengthen opposition to British rule.

All this opposition forced the British government to withdraw the Stamp Act. But it was determined to show the colonists that it had the right to tax them. Parliament passed another law called the Declaratory Act. This stated that the British government had "full power and authority (over) the colonies and people of America in all cases whatsoever."

In 1767 the British placed new taxes on tea, paper, paint, and various other goods that the colonies imported from abroad. A special customs office was set up in Boston to collect the new duties. Again the colonists refused to pay. Riots broke out in Boston and the British sent soldiers to keep order. It was not until 1770, when the British removed all the duties except for the one on tea, that there was less trouble.

But some colonists in Massachusetts were determined to keep the quarrel going. In December 1773, a group of them disguised themselves as Mohawk Amerindians. They boarded British merchant ships in Boston harbor and threw 342 cases of tea into the sea. "I hope that King George likes salt in his tea," said one of them.

The British reply to this "Boston Tea Party" was to pass a set of laws to punish Massachusetts. Colonists soon began calling these laws the "Intolerable Acts." Boston harbor was closed to all trade until the tea was paid for. More soldiers were sent there to keep order. The powers of the colonial assembly of Massachusetts were greatly reduced.

On June 1, 1774, British warships took up position at the mouth of Boston harbor to make sure that no ships sailed in or out. A few months later, in September 1774, a group of colonial leaders came together in Philadelphia. They formed the First Continental Congress to oppose what they saw as British oppression.

The Continental Congress claimed to be loyal to the British king. But it called upon all Americans to support the people of Massachusetts by refusing to buy British goods. Many colonists went further than this. They began to organize themselves into groups of part-time soldiers, or "militias," and to gather together weapons and ammunition.

7
FIGHTING FOR INDEPENDENCE

On the night of April 18, 1775, 700 British soldiers marched silently out of Boston. Their orders were to seize weapons and ammunition that rebellious colonists had stored in Concord, a nearby town.

But the colonists were warned that the soldiers were coming. Signal lights were hung from the spire of Boston's tallest church and two fast riders, Paul Revere and William Dawes, jumped into their saddles and galloped off with the news.

In the village of Lexington the British found seventy American militiamen, farmers and tradesmen, barring their way. These part-time soldiers were known as "Minutemen." This was because they had promised to take up arms immediately – in a minute – whenever they were needed.

The British commander ordered the Minutemen to return to their homes. They refused. Then someone, nobody knows who, fired a shot. Other shots came from the lines of British soldiers. Eight Minutemen fell dead. The first shots had been fired in what was to become the American War of Independence.

The British soldiers reached Concord a few hours later and destroyed some of the weapons and gunpowder there. But by the time they set off to return to Boston hundreds more Minutemen had gathered. From the thick woods on each side of the Boston road they shot down, one by one, 273 British soldiers. The soldiers were still under attack when they arrived back in Boston. A ring of armed Americans gathered round the city.

The next month, May 1775, a second Continental Congress met in Philadelphia and began to act as an American national government. It set up an army of 17,000 men under the command of George Washington. Washington was a Virginia landowner and surveyor with experience of fighting in the French and Indian War. The Continental Congress also sent representatives to seek aid from friendly European nations – especially from France, Britain's old enemy.

British soldiers firing on the Minutemen at Lexington in 1775. A contemporary engraving based on a sketch by an eye-witness.

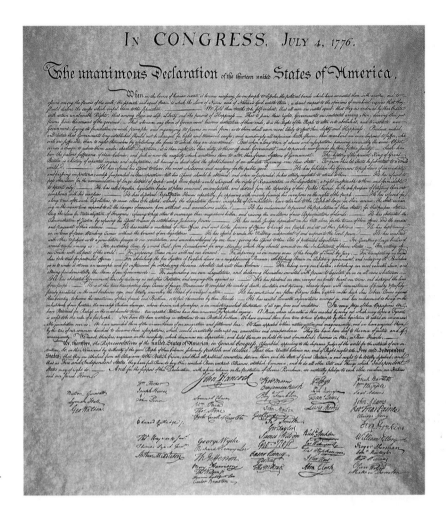

The Declaration of Independence.

By the following year the fighting had spread beyond Massachusetts. It had grown into a full-scale war.

On July 2, 1776, the Continental Congress finally took the step that many Americans believed was inevitable. It cut all political ties with Britain and declared that "these United Colonies are, and of right ought to be, free and independent states." Two days later, on July 4, it issued the *Declaration of Independence*.

The *Declaration of Independence* is the most important document in American history. It was written by Thomas Jefferson, a landowner and lawyer from Virginia. After repeating that the colonies were now "free and independent states." it officially named them the United States of America.

One of the first members of the Continental Congress to sign the *Declaration of Independence* was John Hancock of Massachusetts. Hancock picked up the pen and wrote his name in large, clear letters – "large enough," he said, "for King George to read without his spectacles."

The *Declaration of Independence* was more than a statement that the colonies were a new nation. It also set out the ideas behind the change that was being made. It claimed that all men had a natural right to "Life, liberty and the pursuit of happiness." It also said that governments can only justly claim the right to rule if they have the agreement of those they govern – "the consent of the governed."

Ideas such as these were a central part of the political traditions that the colonists' ancestors had brought with them from England. Colonial leaders had also studied them in the writings of an English political thinker named John Locke. Men like Jefferson combined Locke's ideas with their own experience of

Thomas Paine, the voice of revolution

One of the most influential voices calling for American independence was that of an Englishman. He was a Republican named Thomas Paine, who immigrated to America in 1774.

Two years later, in a brilliantly written pamphlet called *Common Sense*, Paine became one of the first to persuade Americans to make a complete break with Britain. "Everything that is right or reasonable cries for separation," he claimed. "'Tis time to part!"

Common Sense made Paine famous. It had an enormous effect on American opinion and prepared people's minds for independence. It was read on frontier farms and on city streets. Officers read parts of it to their troops. George Washington described its arguments as "sound and unanswerable."

Later in 1776, as Washington's discouraged army retreated from the advancing British, Paine rallied the Americans with a new pamphlet called *The Crisis*. Its words are still remembered in times of difficulty by Americans today. "These are the times that try men's souls," Paine wrote. "The summer soldier and the sunshine patriot will, in this crisis, shrink from the service of his country; but he that stands *now* deserves the love and thanks of man and woman." In one of the darkest hours of the war Paine's words helped to save Washington's armies from melting away and inspired new supporters to join the American cause.

life in America to produce a new definition of democratic government. This new definition said that governments should consist of representatives elected by the people. It also said that the main reason that governments existed was to protect the rights of individual citizens.

After some early successes, the Americans did badly in the war against the British. Washington's army was more of an armed mob than an effective fighting force. Few of the men had any military training and many obeyed only those orders that suited them. Officers quarreled constantly over their rank and

American general Nathan Heard reading the Declaration of Independence *to his troops.*

authority. Washington set to work to train his men and turn them into disciplined soldiers. But this took time, and meanwhile the Americans suffered defeat after defeat. In September 1776, only two months after the *Declaration of Independence*, the British captured New York City. Washington wrote to his brother that he feared that the Americans were very close to losing the war.

Success began to come to the Americans in October 1777. They trapped a British army of almost 6,000 men at Saratoga in northern New York. The British commander was cut off from his supplies and his men were facing starvation. He was forced to surrender. The Americans marched their prisoners to Boston. Here, after swearing never again to fight against the Americans, the prisoners were put on board ships and sent back to England.

Benjamin Franklin, the American ambassador to France, was delighted when he received the news of the victory at Saratoga. He used it to persuade the French government to join in the struggle against Britain. In February 1778, the French king, Louis XVI, signed an alliance with the Americans. French ships, soldiers and money were soon playing an important part in the war.

From 1778 onwards most of the fighting took place in the southern colonies. It was here that the war came to an end. In September 1781, George Washington, leading a combined American and French army, surrounded 8,000 British troops under General Cornwallis at Yorktown, on the coast of Virginia. Cornwallis was worried, but he expected British ships to arrive and rescue or reinforce his army. When ships arrived off Yorktown, however, they were French ones. Cornwallis was trapped. On October 17, 1781, he surrendered his army to Washington. When the news reached London the British Prime Minister, Lord North, threw up his hands in despair. "It is all over!" he cried.

North was right. The British started to withdraw their forces from America and British and American representatives began to discuss peace terms. In the Treaty of Paris, which was signed in September 1783, Britain officially recognized her former colonies as an independent nation. The treaty granted the new United States all of North America from Canada in the north to Florida in the south, and from the Atlantic coast to the Mississippi River.

The Marquis de Lafayette

In 1777 the Marquis de Lafayette, a twenty-year-old French aristocrat, landed in America. He came partly to fight for a new and free society. But he came also to avenge the death of his father, who had died fighting the British in the French and Indian War.

Lafayette served without pay in the American army and became a major-general on the staff of George Washington. In the next four years he fought in many battles, proving himself to be a brave and determined soldier. He won Washington's respect and friendship and played a part in the final defeat of the British at Yorktown in 1781.

When the war ended Lafayette returned to France. There he continued to support American interests. When the French revolution broke out in 1789, political opponents had Lafayette imprisoned and took away his estates. But Lafayette's American friends did not forget him. In 1794 Congress voted him his unclaimed general's pay of $24,424. A few years later it granted him land in Louisiana.

In 1824 the now aging Lafayette returned to visit the United States. The American people greeted him as a hero, a living symbol of the birth of their nation.

The Marquis de Lafayette.

A New Nation

Forming the New Nation

The Treaty of Paris had recognized the United States as an independent nation. But it was not one nation as it is today. In 1783 most Americans felt more loyalty to their own state than to the new United States. They saw themselves first as Virginians or New Yorkers rather than as Americans.

The patriotic symbols of the new nation: Miss Liberty holds the new flag and places the laurel wreath of victory on George Washington's head. The American eagle flies overhead.

Each individual American state had its own government and behaved very much like an independent country. It made its own laws and its own decisions about how to run its affairs. The first big problem that faced the new United States was how to join together these sometimes quarrelsome little countries into one united nation.

During the War of Independence the states had agreed to work together in a national Congress to which each state sent representatives. The agreement that set up this plan for the states to cooperate with one another was called the Articles of Confederation. It had begun to operate in 1781.

Under the Articles of Confederation the central government of the United States was very weak. It was given certain rights, but it had no power to make those rights effective. Congress could vote to set up a United States army and navy, but it could only obtain soldiers and sailors by asking the states for them. It could vote to spend money, but it had no power to collect taxes to raise the money. This caused serious problems. When, for example, Congress needed money to pay debts owed to France, some states refused to pay.

When the War of Independence was over, individual states began to behave more and more like independent nations. Some set up tax barriers against others. New York placed heavy import duties on firewood imported from the neighboring state of Connecticut and on chickens and eggs from another neighbor, New Jersey. In some places states even began fighting one another to decide the ownership of particular pieces of frontier land.

The weakness of its government made it difficult for the new United States to win the respect or the help of foreign nations. The British felt that the American government was so weak that it was not worth dealing with. George III was sure that the Americans would soon be begging to rejoin the British Empire.

Even France, the ally of the Americans during the War of Independence, refused to recognize Congress as a real government. Thomas Jefferson, now the American representative in France, wrote home sadly that the United States was the least important and least respected of all the nations with embassies in Paris.

Many Americans became worried about the future. How could they win the trust of other nations if they refused to pay their debts? How could the country prosper if the states continued to quarrel among themselves? George Washington was usually an optimist. But even he wrote: "I predict the worst consequences from a half-starved, limping government, always moving on crutches and tottering at every step."

It was clear that for the United States to survive there would have to be changes in the Articles of Confederation. In February 1787, Congress asked each state to send delegates to a meeting or "convention," in Philadelphia to talk about such changes. The smallest state, Rhode Island, refused, but the other twelve agreed. The meeting became known as the Constitutional Convention. It began in May 1787, and fifty-five men attended. They chose George Washington to lead their discussions.

The delegates to the Constitutional Convention disagreed about the changes that were needed. Some were anxious to protect the rights of the individual states. At the same time most wanted a stronger central government. All of them were rich men. They believed that a stronger central government would protect their property and business interests.

The original purpose of the Constitutional Convention was simply to revise the Articles of Confederation. But the delegates did more than this. They started afresh and worked out a completely new system of government for the United States. They set out the plan for this government in a document called the *Constitution of the United States*.

The Constitution gave the United States a "federal" system of government. A federal system is one in which the power to rule is shared. A central, or federal, authority has some of it and the rest is in the hands of local authorities in the separate regions that make up the country.

The new Constitution still left the individual state governments with a wide range of powers. But it made the federal government much stronger than before. It gave it the power to collect taxes, to organize armed forces, to make treaties with foreign countries and to control trade of all kinds.

The Constitution made arrangements for the election of a national leader called the President to take charge of the federal government. He would head the "executive" side of the nation's government. It would be his job to run the country's everyday affairs and to see that people obeyed the laws.

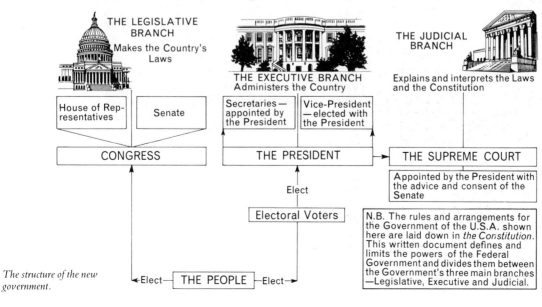

The structure of the new government.

THE LEGISLATIVE BRANCH
Makes the Country's Laws

House of Representatives | Senate

CONGRESS

THE EXECUTIVE BRANCH
Administers the Country

Secretaries — appointed by the President | Vice-President — elected with the President

THE PRESIDENT

THE JUDICIAL BRANCH

Explains and interprets the Laws and the Constitution

THE SUPREME COURT

Appointed by the President with the advice and consent of the Senate

N.B. The rules and arrangements for the Government of the U.S.A. shown here are laid down in *the Constitution*. This written document defines and limits the powers of the Federal Government and divides them between the Government's three main branches —Legislative, Executive and Judicial.

Elect

Electoral Voters

←Elect— THE PEOPLE ⊢Elect→

George Washington and the Whiskey Rebellion

In 1788 George Washington was elected as the first President of the United States. New York was then the country's capital city. On April 30, 1789, Washington stood on a balcony there and swore a solemn oath "to preserve, protect and defend the Constitution of the United States." When the ceremony came to an end he officially took control of the nation's government.

Washington believed that political parties were harmful. He said later that it was "the interest and duty of a wise people to discourage" them. Even so, he favored a strong federal government, so he tended to govern in a Federalist manner. The way that he dealt with the "Whiskey Rebellion" of 1794 was an example of this.

The main crop grown by farmers in western Pennsylvania was corn. Some of this they made into whiskey, which they then sold. When the federal government placed a tax on the whiskey the Pennsylvania farmers refused to pay it. They burned down the houses of the federal tax collectors, or "revenue agents," who tried to make them pay.

Washington sent an army of 15,000 men to support the rights of the federal government. Faced by soldiers, the rebels went home quietly. The Whiskey Rebellion collapsed without any fighting. The soldiers arrested a few of the leaders, but later the President pardoned them.

After this there was no more organized resistance to paying the whiskey tax. But many frontier farmers went on making whiskey that was never taxed. They made it in stills hidden away in the woods, in places that revenue agents could not find. Such illegal "moonshine" whiskey – so called because it was often made at night – continues to be made to this day.

President Washington reviewing the troops at Fort Cumberland, Maryland during the Whiskey Rebellion.

The law-making, or "legislative," powers of the federal government were given to a Congress. This was made up of representatives elected by the people. Congress was to consist of two parts, the Senate and the House of Representatives. In the Senate each state would be equally represented, with two members, whatever the size of its population. The number of representatives a state had in the House of Representatives, however, would depend upon its population.

Finally, the Constitution set up a Supreme Court to control the "judicial" part of the nation's government. The job of the Supreme Court was to make decisions in any disagreements about the meaning of the laws and the Constitution.

The Constitution made sure that there was a "balance of power" between these three main parts, or "branches," of the federal government. To each branch it gave powers that the other two did not have; each had ways of stopping wrongful actions by either of the other two. This was to make sure that no one person or group could become powerful enough to take complete control of the nation's government. The American people had rebelled against being ruled in an undemocratic fashion by Britain. They did not want to replace the unrepresentative rule of the king and parliament in London with the rule of a tyrannical central government in the United States itself.

Many Americans had another fear. This was that the federal government might try to weaken the power of the states to run their own individual affairs. To remove this danger the Constitution said exactly what powers the federal government should have and what powers should be reserved for the states. It said that the states would be allowed to run their internal affairs as they wished, provided that they kept to the rules of the Constitution.

Before the new system of government set out in the Constitution could begin, it had to be approved by a majority of the citizens in at least nine of the thirteen states. People made speeches and wrote newspaper articles both for and against the Constitution. Finally, those in favor won the argument. In June 1788, the assembly of the state of New Hampshire voted to accept, or "ratify," the Constitution. It was the ninth state to do so.

The Constitution went into effect in March 1789. But it was still not really complete. In 1791 ten amendments, or additions, were made to it. Together these ten amendments are called the Bill of Rights.

The reason for the Bill of Rights was that the original Constitution had said nothing about the rights and freedoms of individual citizens. The Bill of Rights altered this. It promised all Americans freedom of religion, a free press, free speech, the right to carry arms, the right to a fair trial by jury, and protection against "cruel and unusual punishments."

In 1801 John Adams, who in 1797 had succeeded George Washington as President of the United States, appointed a new head of the Supreme Court.

The Court's new Chief Justice, to give him his official title, was John Marshall. Marshall was a 46-year-old lawyer and politician who had fought in the American army during the War of Independence.

Marshall was to be Chief Justice of the Supreme Court for thirty-five years. But he made his most important decision as a judge only two years after he was appointed. In an 1803 legal case known as *Marbury* v. *Madison*, Marshall stated that the Supreme Court has the power to decide whether particular American laws are according to the Constitution. If the Supreme Court decides that any law is "repugnant to the Constitution" – that is, does not agree with it – the Court can declare the law illegal, or "void," and so prevent it from being enforced.

This power became known as the "power of judicial review." In claiming it, Marshall established firmly the most important basic idea in American constitutional law. This is, that the Supreme Court is the final authority in deciding the meaning of the Constitution. If its Justices decide that any law is "unconstitutional," that law can no longer be enforced.

The first political parties

The Constitution and the Bill of Rights illustrated two different sides of American political life. On the one hand people saw that the country needed a strong and efficient central authority. On the other hand they wanted to protect individual rights and freedoms. Differing ideas about the importance of these issues gave birth to the first political parties in the United States.

The Federalist Party favored a strong President and federal government. For this reason it appealed to richer people, who believed that a strong central government would make their property safer. The Democratic Republican Party attracted the less wealthy. This was because it supported the rights of the individual states. To people such as small farmers and craftsmen this seemed likely to make it easier for people like themselves to control government actions.

YEARS OF GROWTH

Iroquois warriors attacking settlers.

Land was becoming scarcer and more expensive in the American colonies by the time they quarreled with Britain. After 1783 more and more people set off for the new territories between the Appalachian Mountains and the Mississippi River that the Treaty of Paris had granted to the United States. Armed only with axes, guns, and plenty of self-confidence, they journeyed across the mountains to make new farms and settlements out of the wilderness.

Many of the new settlers moved to lands north of the Ohio River. Amerindians who already lived on these lands saw the settlers as thieves who had come to steal their hunting grounds. They made fierce attacks on the newcomers' farms and settlements. The settlers struck back, sometimes destroying entire Amerindian villages.

The new government of the United States tried at first to keep the peace by making treaties with the Amerindians. It also tried to make sure that settlers treated them fairly. A law of 1787 called the Northwest Ordinance said that the Amerindians' "lands and property shall never be taken from them without their consent; and in their property, rights and liberty they never shall be invaded or disturbed."

But the American government soon changed its ideas about not taking away the Amerindians' "lands and property." By 1817 President James Monroe was writing that their hunting way of life "requires a greater extent of territory than is compatible with the progress of civilized life and must yield to it. If the Indian tribes do not abandon that state and become civilized they will decline and become extinct."

Monroe believed that there was only one way for the Amerindians to survive. They would have to be moved from lands that white settlers wanted to other lands, further west. There, undisturbed by settlers, they would be free either to continue their old ways of life or to adopt those of white Americans.

In 1830 the United States government passed a law called the Indian Removal Act to put this policy into practice. The law said that all Indians living east of the Mississippi River would be moved west to a place called Indian Territory. This was an area beyond the Mississippi that was thought to be unsuitable for white farmers. Some people claimed that the Indian Removal Act was a way of saving the Amerindians. But most saw it simply as a way to get rid of them and seize their land.

The Cherokees were an Amerindian people who suffered greatly from the Indian Removal policy. Their lands lay between the state of Georgia and the Mississippi River. By the early nineteenth century the Cherokees had changed themselves from a stone age tribe into a civilized community.

Old Hickory

The first six Presidents of the United States were all from rich families. Also, all of them came from long-settled states along the Atlantic coast. Then, in 1828, a different sort of President was elected. His name was Andrew Jackson and he had been born into a poor family on the western frontier.

Jackson had commanded the American army at the Battle of New Orleans in 1814. By 1828 he was a rich landowner. But frontier farmers always felt that he was one of them and called him "Old Hickory." Hickory is a particularly tough kind of wood that grows in American forests.

Jackson was one of the founders of the Democratic Party. He said that government should be organized to benefit "the great body of the United States – the planter, the farmer, the mechanic and the laborer." It was the votes of such people that made him President in 1828 and then again in 1832.

Jackson rewarded the people who voted for him by introducing government policies to give them what they wanted. And what they wanted above all were three things – cheap money, cheap manufactured goods and cheap land.

Jackson provided cheap money by encouraging banks to make loans at low rates of interest. He provided cheap manufactured goods by reducing import duties. And he provided cheap land by forcing the Cherokees and other eastern Amerindians to move west of the Mississippi.

Opinions about Jackson's motives are divided. Some believe that he was concerned only about winning popularity and the power that went with it. But others say that his policies of giving voters what they wanted – "Jacksonian democracy" – were an important landmark in making the United States a more genuinely democratic country.

The Trail of Tears – Amerindians driven from their homelands.

Many owned large farms and lived in European-style houses built of brick. They had become Christians and attended church and sent their children to school. Their towns had stores, sawmills and blacksmiths' shops. They had a written language and published their own newspaper in both Cherokee and English. They even wrote for themselves a Constitution modeled on that of the United States.

None of this saved the Cherokees. In the 1830s Congress declared that their lands belonged to the state of Georgia and they were divided up for sale to white settlers. The Cherokees were driven from their homes and forced to march hundreds of miles overland to what is now the state of Oklahoma.

The worst year was 1838. In bitterly cold winter weather American soldiers gathered thousands of Cherokee men, women, and children, and drove them west. The nightmare journey lasted almost five months. By the time it was over, 4,000 of the Amerindians – a quarter of the whole Cherokee nation – were dead. This episode is still remembered with shame by modern Americans. It came to be called "The Trail of Tears."

Long before the Indian Removal Act the federal government had begun to organize the new western lands for settlement. It ordered that the lands should be surveyed and divided into square units called "townships." Each township was to be six miles by six miles in size and each was to be further divided into smaller square units, one mile by one mile, called "sections."

As each township was surveyed and marked out in sections the land was sold by auction. Land dealers sometimes bought whole townships. They usually sold the land later, at a higher price, to settlers arriving from the East.

Every year more settlers moved in. Many floated on rafts down the westward-flowing Ohio River. They used the river as a road to carry themselves, their goods and their animals into the new lands. Others moved west along routes like the Wilderness Road that Daniel Boone's axmen had cut through the Cumberland Gap in the Appalachians. Such roads were simply rough tracks, just wide enough for a wagon and full of holes, rocks and tree stumps. The average speed at which travelers could move along them was about two miles an hour.

Samuel Slater imports the Industrial Revolution

At the end of the War of Independence the United States was mainly a land of farmers. It remained so for another hundred years. It earned its living by selling food and raw materials to other countries. In return it imported their manufactured products. Yet as early as the 1790s America's first factory opened.

During the eighteenth century an Industrial Revolution had come to Britain. New machines driven by water and steam power had made possible great increases in production.

In 1789 an English mechanic named Samuel Slater took the Industrial Revolution across the Atlantic to America. Before leaving England, Slater memorized the details of the latest English cotton spinning machines. He carried them in his memory because it was against the law to take plans of the machines out of England.

In the United States Slater went into partnership with a businessman named Moses Brown. Together they opened a mill, or factory, to spin cotton at Pawtucket, Rhode Island. Slater built the machinery for the mill from memory. It was a great success and Slater became a wealthy man.

The success of Slater's cotton mill began a process of change in the United States. In time that process turned the northeast of the nation into its first important manufacturing region.

The cotton mill at Pawtucket, Rhode Island.

For purposes of government the federal authorities divided the lands between the Appalachians and the Mississippi into two. The Ohio River marked the boundary between them. The area south of the Ohio was called the Southwest Territory and that to the north the Northwest Territory.

As the number of people living in them increased, each of these two big territories was divided again into smaller ones. Ohio, Indiana, Illinois, Michigan, and Wisconsin were eventually made out of the Northwest Territory. As each was formed it was placed under the rule of a governor appointed by Congress. When the number of white males living in a territory reached 5,000 it could elect its own law-making body. It could also send a representative to give its point of view in Congress. When the population of a territory reached 60,000 it became a new state, with the same rights and powers as the original thirteen states.

These arrangements for governing new territories were first introduced by the Northwest Ordinance of 1787. The plan that the Ordinance laid down for controlling the growth of the United States has been followed ever since. The importance of the plan is that it made sure that the original thirteen states were not able to control for their own benefit lands that were settled later. This meant that as the United States grew bigger it went on being a democratic union of equals.

The War of 1812

Between 1803 and 1815 Britain and France were at war. Both countries' warships interfered with American trade. They stopped American merchant ships and sometimes seized their cargoes. Americans became angry. They were especially angry at the British because the British took seamen off American ships and forced them to serve in the British navy.

In June 1812, Congress declared war on Britain. In the early months of this War of 1812 American ships won a number of fights at sea. But the much stronger British navy soon gained complete control of the coastal waters of the United States and blockaded American ports. American attempts to invade British-ruled Canada ended in disaster. Even more humiliating for the Americans, British forces captured and burned Washington, their new capital city.

In December 1814, the United States and Britain signed a treaty of peace in Europe. Two weeks later, before the news reached America, British forces attacked the city of New Orleans. They were defeated by American soldiers led by General Andrew Jackson.

In many ways the whole of the War of 1812 was as pointless as this last battle. But it taught Americans an important lesson. The British navy's wartime

The American ship Constitution *attacking the British ship* Java.

blockade of United States ports had cut off the imported European manufactured goods upon which the country relied. This forced Americans to begin making goods of their own and so gave a start to American manufacturing industry.

Thomas Jefferson was one of many people who had been against the growth of industry in the United States. Now he saw how important it was to the future safety and prosperity of the country. Soon after the War of 1812 he wrote: "We must now place the manufacturer by the side of the agriculturist."

— 10 —
WEST TO THE PACIFIC

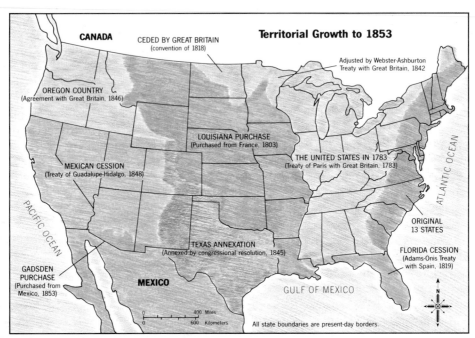

The growth of the U.S.A. (1853).

In 1800 the western boundary of the United States was the Mississippi River. Beyond its wide and muddy waters there were great areas of land through which few white people had traveled. The land stretched west for more than 600 miles to the foothills of the Rocky Mountains. It was known at the time as Louisiana.

In 1800 Louisiana belonged to France. The ruler of France at this time was Napoleon, who would soon become the country's emperor. Americans feared that Napoleon might send French soldiers and settlers to Louisiana and so block the further westward growth of the United States.

Then the Americans were very lucky. In 1803 Napoleon was about to go to war with Britain and needed money. For fifteen million dollars he sold Louisiana to the United States. "We have lived long but this is the noblest work of our whole lives," said one of the American representatives who signed the agreement.

Louisiana stretched north from the Gulf of Mexico to the Canadian border and west from the Mississippi to

the Rocky Mountains. Its purchase almost doubled the land area of the United States. In time, all or parts of thirteen new states would be formed there.

The Louisiana Purchase was authorized by President Thomas Jefferson. Even before this Jefferson had been planning to send an expedition to explore Louisiana. He was a keen amateur scientist and wanted to know more about the geography, the people, the animals and the plants of the lands to the west of the United States. He also hoped that the explorers might find an easy way across North America to the Pacific Ocean.

The expedition was led by Meriwether Lewis and William Clark. In the spring of 1804 its twenty-nine men left the trading post of St. Louis, where the Missouri River flows in from the northwest to meet the Mississippi. The explorers set off up the Missouri by boat. Among their supplies they carried 4,600 needles, 2,800 fishing hooks, 132 knives and 72 pieces of striped silk ribbon. They carried these goods to trade with Amerindians along the way.

For months the explorers rowed and sailed their boats up the Missouri, hoping that it would lead them to the Pacific. Sometimes they had to wade shoulder-deep in the river, pulling the boats forward against fast and dangerous currents. When the Missouri became too shallow to follow any further, they marched for ten weeks across the Rocky Mountains, killing their horses for food and with only melted snow to drink. At last they reached the westward-flowing Columbia River. They floated down it to the Pacific. On a pine tree growing by the shore Clark carved a message – "Will. Clark, Dec. 3, 1805. By land from the United States in 1804 and 1805."

Lewis and Clark arrived back in St. Louis in late September 1806. They had been away for two and a half years and had traveled almost 4,000 miles. They had failed to find an easy overland route to the Pacific, but they had shown that the journey was possible. They had also brought back much useful information about both Louisiana and the western lands that lay beyond it.

These lands beyond Louisiana were known as Oregon. They stretched from Alaska in the north to California in the south and inland through the Rocky Mountains to the undefined borders of Louisiana. In 1805 four countries claimed to own Oregon – Russia, Spain, Britain and the United States.

Russia owned Alaska, and Spain ruled California. But in Oregon the British and the Americans were in the strongest position. Both already had trading posts scattered along Oregon's coasts and rivers. Soon they had more. At these posts traders bought beaver and other animal furs from Amerindian and European trappers. Such trappers were called "mountain-men" because they spent their lives wandering the mountains of Oregon and California in search of furs.

By the 1830s the British had more settlements and trading posts in Oregon than the Americans. American political leaders began to fear that Britain would soon gain complete control of the area. To prevent this they made great efforts to persuade more Americans to start farms in Oregon.

At first Americans traveling to Oregon went by ship. They sailed from the east coast ports of the United States, around South America and up the long Pacific coast. The journey was expensive and it lasted for months. Settlers began traveling to Oregon by land in 1832. They usually set out from Independence,

*Amerindians discovering
Lewis and Clark.*

Zebulon Pike and the Great American Desert

While Lewis and Clark were crossing the plains and mountains of the American Northwest, another expedition was exploring those of the Southwest. The leader of the expedition was a young lieutenant in the American army named Zebulon M. Pike.

In November 1806, Pike and his men reached the Rocky Mountains near where the city of Pueblo, Colorado, now stands. The following spring Pike traveled further into the mountains, into lands that were then ruled by Spain. Eventually he was arrested by Spanish soldiers. Although the Spaniards treated him with courtesy, they took away his notes and papers and sent him back to the United States.

Pike is remembered today for two things. One is Pikes Peak, a high mountain in Colorado which he first sighted on November 15, 1806, and which is named after him. The other is for his opinion that the entire central region of North America between the Mississippi and the Rockies was little better than a desert and "incapable of cultivation."

For years after Pike's journey this area was described on maps as "The Great American Desert." But both Pike and the mapmakers were wrong. By the 1870s improved seeds and better methods of cultivation were making it possible for farmers to turn these lands into one of the richest grain-growing areas in the world.

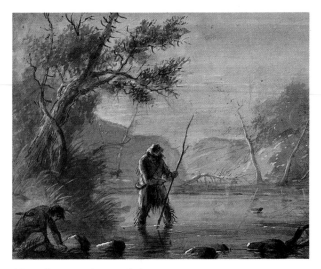

Mountain-men setting traps for beaver.

Settlers faced many dangers on the way to Oregon. Floods and blizzards, prairie fires and accidents, disease and starvation – all these took many lives. One settler recorded in his diary a common sight along the trail: "At noon came upon a fresh grave with a note tied on a stick, informing us it was the grave of Joel Hembree, aged six years, killed by a wagon running over his body."

But, in spite of the dangers, settlers continued to make the long journey. In 1843 "Oregon fever" came to many parts of the United States. People left their worn-out farms in the East, packed their possessions on wagons and set off for the West. "I have seen hard times, faced the dangers of disease and exposure and perils of all kinds," wrote one, "but I do not care about them if they enable me to place myself and my family in comfortable circumstances [better conditions]."

American settlers soon outnumbered the British in Oregon. American newspapers and political leaders began to express an idea called "manifest destiny." This was a claim that it was the clear ("manifest") intention of fate ("destiny") that the territory of the United States should stretch across North America from the Atlantic to the Pacific. Supporters of manifest destiny demanded that the United States should take the whole of Oregon, all the way north to the boundary with Alaska at latitude 54 degrees 40 minutes. They began using the slogan "Fifty four forty or fight" and threatened the British with war.

Missouri, a town on the Mississippi River. From Independence they followed a twisting trail of about 2,000 miles across plains and mountains to the mouth of the Columbia River.

This overland route to the Pacific coast became known as the Oregon Trail. The wheels of the wagons that traveled along it made deep ruts. These ruts can still be seen in dry areas of the American West today. But the Oregon Trail was never a single trail. It was more a collection of trails, all heading in the same general direction across western North America and meeting occasionally at river-crossing points and passes through the mountains.

In 1844 James K. Polk was elected President of the United States. Polk believed strongly in manifest destiny. In the speech at the start of his presidency – his "inaugural" address – he said that the American claim "to the whole of Oregon is clear and unquestionable." For a time war seemed possible.

But by the summer of 1846 the United States was already at war with Mexico. In June Polk agreed to divide Oregon with Britain in two almost equal sections. The dividing line was the 49th parallel of latitude, which already formed the boundary between the United States and Canada to the east of the Rocky Mountains.

The 1846 war with Mexico had grown out of events that had been taking place in Texas. Thousands of Americans had settled in Texas, but up to the 1830s it was ruled by Mexico. The Texas Americans, or Texans, came to dislike Mexican rule. In October 1835, they rebelled. Led by General Sam Houston, they defeated a much larger Mexican army in 1836 at the Battle of San Jacinto and made Texas an independent republic.

But most Texans did not want their independence to be permanent. They wanted their country to join the United States. Eventually the two countries reached an agreement about this and in 1845 Texas became part of the United States.

In April 1846, there was fighting between American and Mexican soldiers along the border between Texas and Mexico. President Polk saw an opportunity to take land from Mexico and he declared war. American soldiers invaded Mexico and defeated the Mexican army. By September 1847, they had occupied Mexico City, the country's capital.

The Mexican-American War was ended by a peace treaty signed in February 1848. The treaty forced Mexico to hand over enormous stretches of its territory to the United States. Today these lands form the American states of California, Arizona, Nevada, Utah, New Mexico and Colorado.

The annexation of these Mexican lands completed the "manifest destiny" of the United States. It now stretched across the North American continent from ocean to ocean. In little more than half a century it had grown from a small nation on the shores of the Atlantic into one of the largest countries in the world.

Wagon trains

Most of the settlers who traveled to Oregon made the journey in four-wheeled wagons. A group of these wagons traveling together was called a "wagon train." A wagon train usually consisted of about twenty-five wagons, each with a canvas cover to protect its contents from the weather. Seen from a distance, these covers made the wagons look like ships sailing across a sea of grass. Because of this, people often called wagons "prairie schooners." A schooner was a type of sailing ship.

Each wagon could carry a load of between 2 and 2½ tons and was pulled by a team of either mules or oxen. Settlers argued fiercely about which animals were better. Some claimed that mules were faster and tougher than oxen. Others argued that oxen were stronger than mules and easier to control. Some people believe that the phrase "as stubborn as a mule" became part of the English language at this time.

Cost usually settled the arguments. A settler could buy three oxen for the price of only one mule. For this reason oxen were used more than any other animals to pull the wagons that traveled the Oregon Trail.

A wagon train crossing the prairie.

11
NORTH AND SOUTH

Slaves preparing the ground to plant cotton on a southern plantation.

In the year 1810 there were 7.2 million people in the United States. For 1.2 million of these people the words of the *Declaration of Independence* "that all men are created equal" were far from true. They were black and they were slaves.

Thomas Jefferson, who wrote the *Declaration of Independence*, owned slaves himself. So did George Washington and other leaders of the movement for American independence and freedom. Both Jefferson and Washington had uneasy consciences about this. But other big landowners in southern states such as Virginia defended slavery. They asked what they thought was an unanswerable question. How could they cultivate their fields of tobacco, rice and cotton without slave workers?

In the north of the United States farms were smaller and the climate was cooler. Farmers there did not need slaves to work the land for them. Some northerners opposed slavery for moral and religious reasons also. Many were abolitionists – that is, people who wanted to end or abolish slavery by law. By the early nineteenth century many northern states had passed laws abolishing slavery inside their own boundaries. In 1808 they also persuaded Congress to make it illegal for ships to bring any new slaves from Africa into the United States.

By the 1820s southern and northern politicians were arguing fiercely about whether slavery should be permitted in the new territories that were then being settled in the West. The argument centered on the

Missouri territory, which was part of the Louisiana Purchase. Southerners argued that slave labor should be allowed in Missouri and all the other lands that formed part of the Louisiana Purchase. Both abolitionists and other northerners objected strongly to this. Northern farmers moving west did not want to find themselves competing for land against southerners who had slaves to do their work for them. Eventually the two sides agreed on a compromise. Slavery would be permitted in the Missouri and Arkansas territories but banned in lands to the west and north of Missouri. ✗

The Missouri Compromise, as it was called, did not end the disputes between North and South. By the early 1830s another angry argument was going on. This time the argument began over import duties. Northern states favored such duties because they protected their young industries against the competition of foreign manufactured goods. Southern states opposed them because southerners relied upon foreign manufacturers for both necessities and luxuries of many kinds. Import duties would raise the prices of such goods.

During the argument about import duties a southern political leader named John C. Calhoun raised a much more serious question. He claimed that a state had the right to disobey any federal law if the state believed that the law would harm its interests. This

idea was strongly supported by other southerners. It became known as the "states' rights doctrine."

Calhoun's claim was strongly denied by Senator Daniel Webster of Massachusetts. The power to decide whether the federal authorities were acting rightly or wrongly belonged to the Supreme Court, said Webster, not to individual states. If states were given the right to disobey the federal government, he said, it would become "a mere rope of sand" and lose its power to hold the country together. Webster's speech was a warning to Americans that the states' rights doctrine could become a serious threat to the unity of the United States.

In the next twenty years the United States grew much bigger. In 1846 it divided the Oregon Territory with Britain. In 1848 it took vast areas of the Southwest from Mexico. Obtaining these new lands raised again the question that the Missouri Compromise of 1820 had tried to settle – should slavery be allowed on new American territory? Once again southerners answered "yes." And once again northerners said "no."

In 1850 Congress voted in favor of another compromise. California was admitted to the United States as a free state, while people who lived in Utah and New Mexico were given the right to decide for themselves whether or not to allow slavery.

Harvest time on a cotton plantation beside the Mississippi River.

Eli Whitney and the cotton gin

In 1793 a young school teacher named Eli Whitney was visiting friends in the southern state of Georgia. Like other states in the South, Georgia's main crop was cotton. Georgia's planters exported their cotton to spinning mills in England. However, the mills could not use Georgia's cotton until its growers removed the many seeds that were tangled among its fibers. This was a slow and difficult job that was done by hand. Until a way could be found to do it more quickly, the amount of cotton that planters grew was limited to the amount that their workers could pick the seeds from.

Eli Whitney had a talent for making machines. He solved the planters' problem by inventing the cotton "engine" – or "gin" for short. This was a machine that quickly separated the seeds and the fiber of the raw cotton. Using Whitney's gin, one worker could remove the seeds from more than four hundred pounds of cotton in the same time that it had taken previously to remove them from two pounds.

Whitney's invention made possible a huge increase in the amount of cotton grown by southern planters. By the year 1820 the output of their plantations and farms was eight thousand times higher than in 1791. The increase was achieved by bringing in more slaves to plough and hoe the land and pick the cotton. The prosperity of the planters came to depend more every year on slavery being allowed to continue.

This fact, more perhaps than any other, explains why southerners broke away from the rest of the United States. They did so in order to try to save slavery – their "peculiar institution" as they called it – and with it their prosperity and way of life.

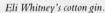

Eli Whitney's cotton gin.

To persuade southerners to agree to these arrangements, Congress passed a new Fugitive Slave Act. This was a law to make it easier for southerners to recapture slaves who escaped from their masters and fled for safety to free states. The law called for "severe penalties on anyone assisting Negroes to escape from bondage."

Slave owners had long offered rewards, or "bounties," for the return of runaway slaves. This had created a group of men called "bounty hunters." These men made their living by hunting down fugitive slaves in order to collect the rewards on them. With the support of the new law, bounty hunters now began searching free states for escaped slaves.

The Fugitive Slave Act angered many northerners who had not so far given much thought to the rights and wrongs of slavery. Some northern judges refused to enforce it. Other people provided food, money, and hiding places for fugitives. They mapped out escape routes and moved runaway slaves by night from one secret hiding place to another. The final stop on these escape routes was Canada, where fugitives could be followed by neither American laws nor bounty hunters.

Because railroads were the most modern form of transport at this time, this carefully organized system was called the "Underground Railroad." People providing money to pay for it were called "stockholders." Guides who led the fugitives to freedom were called "conductors," and hiding places were called "depots." All these were terms that were used on ordinary railroads.

Many conductors on the Underground Railroad were former slaves themselves. Often they traveled deep into slave states to make contact with runaways. This was a dangerous thing to do. If conductors were captured they could end up as slaves again – or dead. As the number of fugitive slaves increased, gunfights between bounty hunters and conductors became more and more common.

In 1854 a Senator named Stephen Douglas persuaded Congress to end the Missouri Compromise. West of Missouri, on land that was supposed to be closed to slavery, was a western territory called Kansas. In 1854 Congress voted to let its people decide for themselves whether to permit slavery there.

William Lloyd Garrison and the abolitionists

Some Americans opposed to slavery were prepared to wait for it to come to an end gradually and by agreement with the slave owners. Others wanted to end it immediately and without compromises. The best known spokesman of the people in this second group was a Boston writer named William Lloyd Garrison.

On January 1, 1831, Garrison produced the first issue of *The Liberator*, a newspaper dedicated to the abolition of slavery. "On this subject I do not wish to think, or speak, or write with moderation," he wrote. "I will not retreat a single inch – and I will be heard."

Garrison meant what he said. He became well-known for the extreme way in which he expressed his views. He printed, and sometimes invented, sensational stories about how cruelly black slaves were treated. He attacked slave owners as evil monsters, about whom nothing good could be said.

Sometimes Garrison went too far even for his fellow northerners. In 1835 an angry mob showed its dislike of his opinions by parading him through the streets of Boston with a rope around his neck. But Garrison refused to be silenced. His blood-thirsty calls for action and sensational stories continued to offend both the supporters of slavery and those who wanted to bring it to an end peacefully. But they convinced many other people that slavery was evil and that it must be abolished at once – even if the only way to do this was by war.

A race began to win control of Kansas. Pro-slavery immigrants poured in from the South and anti-slavery immigrants from the North. Each group was determined to outnumber the other. Soon fighting and killing began. Pro-slavery raiders from Missouri burned a town called Lawrence and killed some of its people. In reply, a half-mad abolitionist named John Brown led a raid in which a number of supporters of slavery were killed. Because of all the fighting and killing in the territory Americans everywhere began referring to it as "bleeding Kansas."

Dred Scott.

Neither side won the struggle to control Kansas in the 1850s. Because of the trouble there, Congress delayed its admission to the United States. But in 1858 the supporters of slavery won a victory of another sort.

A slave named Dred Scott had been taken by his owner to live in a free state. Scott asked the Supreme Court to declare that this had made him legally free. But the Court refused. It said that black slaves had no rights as American citizens. It added also that Congress had gone beyond its constitutional powers in claiming the right to prohibit slavery in the western territories.

The Dred Scott decision caused great excitement in the United States. Southern slave owners were delighted. Opponents of slavery were horrified. The Supreme Court seemed to be saying that free states had no right to forbid slavery within their boundaries and that slave owners could put their slaves to work anywhere.

A few years earlier opponents of slavery had formed a new political group called the Republican Party.

When Senator Stephen Douglas asked the voters of Illinois to re-elect him to Congress in 1858, he was challenged by a Republican named Abraham Lincoln. In a series of public debates with Douglas, Lincoln said that the spread of slavery must be stopped. He was willing to accept slavery in the states where it existed already, but that was all. Looking to the future of the United States he gave his listeners a warning. "A house divided against itself cannot stand. I believe that this government cannot endure permanently half slave and half free."

Lincoln lost the 1858 election to Douglas. But his stand against slavery impressed many people. In 1860 the Republicans chose him as their candidate in that year's presidential election.

By now relations between North and South were close to breaking point. In 1859 the same John Brown who had fought in "bleeding Kansas" had tried to start a slave rebellion in Virginia. He attacked an army weapons store at a place called Harpers Ferry. The attack failed and Brown was captured, tried for treason and hanged. But that was not the end of John Brown. Many northerners claimed that he was a martyr in the struggle against slavery. They even wrote a song about him. "John Brown's body lies a-moldering in the grave," they sang, "but his soul goes marching on."

Southerners saw the raid on Harpers Ferry differently. They believed that it was a sign that the North was preparing to use force to end slavery in the South. In the presidential election of 1860 the southerners put forward a candidate of their own to oppose Lincoln. They threatened that the South would break away, or "secede," from the United States if Lincoln became President.

In every southern state a majority of the citizens voted against Lincoln. But voters in the North supported him and he won the election. A few weeks later, in December 1860, the state of South Carolina voted to secede from the United States. It was soon joined by ten more southern states. In February 1861, these eleven states announced that they were now an independent nation, the Confederate States of America, often known as the Confederacy.

The nineteenth century's bloodiest war, the American Civil War, was about to begin.

Slaves being helped to freedom by the Underground Railroad.

Harriet Tubman

The most famous "conductor" on the Underground Railroad was a young black woman named Harriet Tubman. She was born in 1821 and grew up as a slave on a plantation in Maryland. In 1849 she escaped to Philadelphia and joined the Underground Railroad. Although she could neither read nor write, Harriet Tubman had great abilities as an organizer. Over the next ten years she made nineteen trips into slave states and led more than 300 men, women and children to freedom. On her early trips she led the fugitives to safety in such northern cities as New York and Philadelphia. When the Fugitive Slave Act of 1850 made those cities unsafe, she led the people in her care to Canada.

During the Civil War Harriet Tubman worked as a nurse, a cook and a laundress with the Union armies fighting in the South. It is also said that she risked her life by traveling behind Confederate lines as a spy.

After the Civil War Harriet Tubman lived in Auburn, New York. Here she worked to help children and old people, using the profits she earned from her autobiography to pay for her work. When she died in 1913, she had already become a legend.

12
THE CIVIL WAR

On March 4, 1861, Abraham Lincoln took the oath of office as President of the United States. Less than a month had passed since the formation of the Confederacy. In his inaugural address as President, Lincoln appealed to the southern states to stay in the Union. He promised that he would not interfere with slavery in any of them. But he warned that he would not allow them to break up the United States by seceding. Quoting from his oath of office, he told them: "You have no oath registered in Heaven to destroy the government, while I have a most solemn one to 'preserve, protect and defend' it."

The southern states took no notice of Lincoln's appeal. On April 12 Confederate guns opened fire on Fort Sumter, a fortress in the harbor of Charleston, South Carolina, that was occupied by United States troops. These shots marked the beginning of the American Civil War.

Confederate soldiers.

Lincoln called for 75,000 men to fight to save the Union. Jefferson Davis, the newly elected President of the Confederate States, made a similar appeal for men to fight for the Confederacy. Volunteers rushed forward in thousands on both sides.

Some people found it difficult and painful to decide which side to support. The decision sometimes split families. The son of the commander of the Confederate navy was killed fighting in a Union ship. Two brothers became generals – but on opposite sides. And three of President Lincoln's own brothers-in-law died fighting for the Confederacy.

From the first months of the war Union warships blockaded the ports of the South. They did this to prevent the Confederacy from selling its cotton abroad and from obtaining foreign supplies.

In both men and material resources the North was much stronger than the South. It had a population of twenty-two million people. The South had only nine million people and 3.5 million of them were slaves. The North grew more food crops than the South. It also had more than five times the manufacturing capacity, including most of the country's weapon factories. So the North not only had more fighting men than the South, it could also keep them better supplied with weapons, clothing, food and everything else they needed.

However, the North faced one great difficulty. The only way it could win the war was to invade the South and occupy its land. The South had no such problem. It did not need to conquer the North to win independence. All it had to do was to hold out until the people of the North grew tired of fighting. Most southerners believed that the Confederacy could do this. It began the war with a number of advantages. Many of the best officers in the pre-war army of the United States were southerners. Now they returned to the Confederacy to organize its armies. Most of the recruits led by these officers had grown up on farms and were expert riders and marksmen. Most important of all, the fact that almost all the war's fighting took place in the South meant that Confederate soldiers were defending their own homes. This often made them fight with more spirit than the Union soldiers.

Southerners denied that they were fighting mainly to preserve slavery. Most were poor farmers who owned no slaves anyway. The South was fighting for its independence from the North, they said, just as their grandfathers had fought for independence from Britain almost a century earlier.

The war was fought in two main areas – in Virginia and the other east coast states of the Confederacy, and in the Mississippi valley.

In Virginia the Union armies suffered one defeat after another in the first year of the war. Again and again they tried to capture Richmond, the Confederate capital. Each time they were thrown back with heavy losses. The Confederate forces in Virginia had two great advantages. The first was that many rivers cut across the roads leading south to Richmond and so made the city easier to defend. The second was their leaders. Two Confederate generals in particular, Robert E. Lee and Thomas J. ("Stonewall") Jackson, showed much more skill than the generals leading the Union army at this time. Jackson got his nickname "Stonewall" because he stood firm against advancing Union troops. A fellow officer, encouraging his soldiers shouted out, "Look, there is Jackson, standing like a stone wall!"

The North's early defeats in Virginia discouraged its supporters. The flood of volunteers for the army began to dry up. Recruitment was not helped by letters home like this one, from a lieutenant in the Union army in 1862:

"The butchery of the boys, the sufferings of the unpaid soldiers, without tents, poor rations, a single blanket each, with no bed but the hard damp ground – it is these things that kill me."

Fortunately for the North, Union forces in the Mississippi valley had more success. In April 1862, a naval officer named David Farragut sailed Union ships into the mouth of the river and captured New Orleans, the largest city in the Confederacy. At the same time other Union forces were fighting their way down the Mississippi from the north.

By spring 1863, the Union armies were closing in on an important Confederate stronghold on the Mississippi called Vicksburg. On July 4, after much bloody fighting and a siege lasting six weeks, Vicksburg surrendered to a Union army led by General Ulysses S. Grant. Its fall was a heavy blow to the South. Union forces now controlled the whole length of the Mississippi. They had split the Confederacy in two. It became impossible for western Confederate states like Texas to send any more men and supplies to the east.

But by 1863 many northerners were tired of the war. They were sickened by its heavy cost in lives and money. General Lee, the Confederate commander, believed that if his army could win a decisive victory on northern soil, popular opinion there might force the Union government to make peace.

In the last week of June 1863, Lee marched his army north into Pennsylvania. At a small town named Gettysburg a Union army blocked his way. The battle which followed was the biggest that has ever been fought in the United States. In three days of fierce fighting more than 50,000 men were killed or wounded. On the fourth day Lee broke off the battle and led his men back into the South. The Confederate army had suffered a defeat from which it would never recover.

The Emancipation Proclamation

By the summer of 1862 President Lincoln realized that the North would only win the war if he could arouse more enthusiasm for its cause. On September 22 he issued the Emancipation Proclamation with this aim. This Proclamation declared that from January 1, 1863, all slaves were to be made free – but only if they lived in areas that were part of the Confederacy. The Proclamation changed the purpose of the war. From a struggle to preserve the Union, it became a struggle both to preserve the Union and to abolish slavery.

At the time not everyone was impressed by Lincoln's action. A British leader, Lord Palmerston, said that all Lincoln had done was "to abolish slavery where he was without power to do so, while protecting it where he had the power to destroy it." Palmerston was right. But after the Emancipation Proclamation everyone knew that it was only a matter of time now before slavery was ended everywhere in the United States.

The Battle of Gettysburg.

By 1864 the Confederacy was running out of almost everything – men, equipment, food, money. As fall colored the trees of the eastern woods, the Union armies moved in to end the war. In November 1864, a Union army led by General William T. Sherman began to march through the Confederate state of Georgia. Its soldiers destroyed everything in their path. They tore up railroad tracks, burned crops and buildings, drove off cattle. On December 22 they occupied the city of Savannah. The Confederacy was split again, this time from east to west. After capturing Savannah, Sherman turned north. He marched through the Carolinas, burning and destroying again as he made for Richmond.

The Confederate capital was already in danger from another Union army led by General Grant. By March 1865, Grant had almost encircled the city and on April 2 Lee was forced to abandon it to save his army from being trapped. He marched south, hoping to fight on from a strong position in the mountains. But Grant followed close behind and other Union soldiers blocked Lee's way forward. Lee was trapped. On April 9, 1865, he met Grant in a house in a tiny village called Appomattox and surrendered his army.

Grant treated the defeated Confederate soldiers generously. After they had given up their weapons and promised never again to fight against the United States, he allowed them to go home. He told them they could keep their horses "to help with the spring ploughing." As Lee rode away, Grant stood in the doorway chewing a piece of tobacco and told his men: "The war is over. The rebels are our countrymen again."

The Civil War gave final answers to two questions that had divided the United States ever since it became an independent nation. It put an end to slavery. In 1865 this was abolished everywhere in the United States by the 13th Amendment to the Constitution. And it decided finally that the United States was one nation, whose parts could not be separated.

But the war left bitter memories. The United States fought other wars later, but all were outside its own boundaries. The Civil War caused terrible destruction at home. All over the South cities and farms lay in ruins. And more Americans died in this war than in any other, before or since. By the time Lee surrendered to Grant at Appomattox, the dead on both sides totaled 635,000.

The Gettysburg Address

Gettysburg in Pennsylvania is remembered for two things. The first is the battle that was fought there in July 1863. The second is the Gettysburg address, a speech that Abraham Lincoln made there a few months later.

On November 19, 1863, Lincoln traveled to Gettysburg to dedicate part of the battlefield as a national war cemetery. This is part of what he said when he did so:

"Fourscore and seven years ago our fathers brought forth on this continent a new nation, dedicated to the proposition that all men are created equal. Now we are engaged in a great civil war, testing whether that nation can long endure. We are met on a great battlefield of that war. We have come to dedicate a portion of that field as a final resting-place for those who here gave their lives, that that nation might live. But in a larger sense, we can not dedicate, we can not consecrate this ground. The brave men, living and dead, who struggled here, have consecrated it, far above our poor power. The world will little note, nor long remember, what we say here, but it can never forget what they did here. It is for us the living to resolve that these dead shall not have died in vain; that this nation, under God, shall have a new birth of freedom; and that government of the people, by the people, for the people, shall not perish from this earth."

Lincoln's speech at Gettysburg became even more famous than the battle. At the time it was seen as a statement of what the North was fighting for. In later years it came to be seen as a moving expression of faith in the basic principles of democratic government.

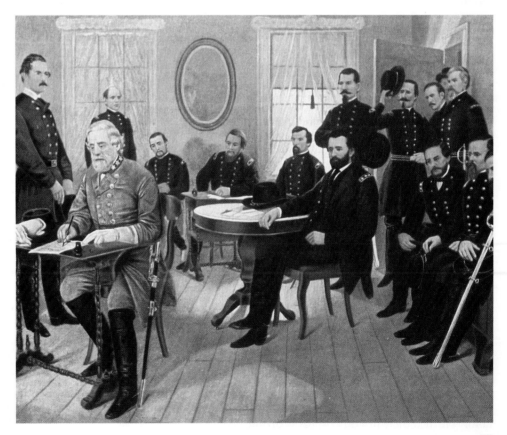

Lee's surrender to Grant at Appomattox in 1865. Grant sits at the table behind Lee in this contemporary painting.

13

RECONSTRUCTION

The assassination of President Lincoln.

On the night of April 13, 1865, crowds of people moved through the brightly lit streets of Washington to celebrate Lee's surrender at Appomattox. A man who was there wrote in his diary: "Guns are firing, bells ringing, flags flying, men laughing, children cheering, all, all are jubilant."

The next day was Good Friday. In the evening President Lincoln and his wife went to Ford's Theater in Washington to see a play called "Our American Cousin." The theater was full and the audience cheered the President as he took his seat in a box beside the stage. Once Lincoln was safely in his seat, his bodyguards moved away to watch the play themselves from seats in the gallery.

At exactly 10:13, when the play was part way through, a pistol shot rang through the darkened theater. As the President slumped forward in his seat, a man in a black felt hat and high boots jumped from the box on to the stage. He waved a gun in the air and shouted "Sic semper tyrannis" [Thus always to tyrants] and then ran out of the theater. It was discovered later that the gunman was an actor named John Wilkes Booth. He was captured a few days later, hiding in a barn in the Virginia countryside.

Lincoln was carried across the street to the house of a tailor. He died there in a downstairs bedroom the

next morning. Men and women wept in the streets when they heard the news. The poet James Russell Lowell wrote: "Never before that startled April morning did such multitudes of men shed tears for the death of one they had never seen, as if with him a friendly presence had been taken from their lives."

Lincoln was succeeded as President by his Vice President, Andrew Johnson. The biggest problem the new President faced was how to deal with the defeated South. Lincoln had made no secret of his own ideas about this. Only a few weeks before his death he had begun his second term of office as President. In his inaugural address he had asked the American people to help him to "bind up the nation's wounds" and rebuild their war-battered homeland.

Lincoln blamed individual southern leaders for the war, rather than the people of the seceding states as a whole. He intended to punish only those guilty individuals and to let the rest of the South's people play a full part in the nation's life again.

Johnson had similar ideas. He began to introduce plans to reunite the South with the rest of the nation. He said that as soon as the citizens of the seceded states promised to be loyal to the government of the United States they could elect new state assemblies to run their affairs. When a state voted to accept the 13th Amendment to the Constitution (the one that completely abolished slavery) Johnson intended that it should be accepted back into the Union as a full and equal member.

But white southerners were determined to resist any changes that threatened their power to control the life of the South. They were especially horrified at the idea of giving equal rights to their former black slaves. The assembly of the state of Mississippi expressed the way it felt in these blunt words:

"Under the pressure of federal bayonets the people of Mississippi have abolished the institution of slavery. The negro is free whether we like it or not. To be free, however, does not make him a citizen or entitle him to social or political equality with the white man."

54

O Captain! my Captain!

Walt Whitman is perhaps the most famous American poet of the nineteenth century. During the Civil War he worked in military hospitals, helping to take care of wounded soldiers. Whitman was a great admirer of Lincoln and in 1865 he expressed his grief at the death of the President by writing this poem. The "fearful trip" in the opening line is the Civil War, the "Captain" is Abraham Lincoln, the "ship" is the United States and the "prize" is peace and national unity.

O Captain! my Captain! our fearful trip is
  done,
The ship has weather'd every rack, the prize
  we sought is won,
The port is near, the bells I hear, the people all
  exulting,
While follow eyes the steady keel, the vessel
  grim and daring;
But O heart! heart! heart!
O the bleeding drops of red,
Where on the deck my Captain lies,
Fallen cold and dead.

O Captain! my Captain! rise up and hear the
  bells;
Rise up – for you the flag is flung – for you the
  bugle trills,
For you bouquets and ribbon'd wreaths – for
  you the shores a-crowding,

For you they call, the swaying mass, their
  eager faces turning;
Here Captain! dear father!
This arm beneath your head!
It is some dream that on the deck,
You've fallen cold and dead.

My Captain does not answer, his lips are pale
  and still,
My father does not feel my arm, he has no
  pulse nor will,
The ship is anchor'd safe and sound, its
  voyage closed and done,
From fearful trip the victor ship comes in
  with object won;
Exult O shores, and ring O bells!
But I with mournful tread,
Walk the deck my Captain lies,
Fallen cold and dead.

Walt Whitman

The other former Confederate states shared this attitude. All their assemblies passed laws to keep blacks in an inferior position. Such laws were called "Black Codes." "Federal bayonets" might have made the blacks free, but the ruling whites intended them to remain unskilled, uneducated and landless, with no legal protection or rights of their own.

Black Codes refused blacks the vote, said that they could not serve on juries, forbade them to give evidence in court against a white man. In Mississippi blacks were not allowed to buy or to rent farm land. In Louisiana they had to agree to work for one employer for a whole year and could be imprisoned and made to do forced labor if they refused. With no land, no money and no protection from the law, it was almost as if blacks were still slaves.

In 1865 the *Chicago Tribune* newspaper warned southerners of the growing anger in the North about the Black Codes:

"We tell the white men of Mississippi that the men of the North will convert the State of Mississippi into a frog pond before they will allow such laws to disgrace one foot of soil in which the bones of our soldiers sleep and over which the flag of freedom waves."

The feelings of the *Chicago Tribune* were shared by many members of the United States Congress. A group there called Radical Republicans believed that the most important reason for fighting the Civil War had been to free the blacks. Having won the war, they were determined that neither they nor the blacks were now going to be cheated. They said that President Johnson was treating the defeated white southerners too kindly and that the southerners were taking advantage of this. "They have not been punished as they deserve," said one Radical Republican.

In July 1866, despite opposition from the President, Congress passed a Civil Rights Act. It also set up an organization called the Freedmen's Bureau. Both these measures were intended to ensure that blacks in the South were not cheated of their rights. Congress then introduced the 14th Amendment to the Constitution. The 14th Amendment gave blacks full rights of citizenship, including the right to vote.

All the former Confederate states except Tennessee refused to accept the 14th Amendment. In March 1867, Congress replied by passing the Reconstruction Act. This dismissed the white governments of the southern states and placed them under military rule. They were told that they could again have elected governments when they accepted the 14th Amendment and gave all black men the vote.

By 1870 all the southern states had new "Reconstruction" governments. Most were made up of blacks, a few white southerners who were willing to work with them and white men from the North.

Blacks voting for the first time after the 14th Amendment.

The newly arrived northerners were referred to by southerners who opposed them as "carpetbaggers." The name came from the large, cheap bags made of carpeting material in which some of the northerners carried their belongings. Any white southerners who cooperated with the carpetbaggers were referred to with contempt as "scalawags." The word "scalawag" still means scoundrel, or rogue, in the English language today.

Most white southerners supported the Democratic political party. These southern Democrats claimed that the Reconstruction governments were incompetent and dishonest. There was some truth in this claim. Many of the new black members of the state assemblies were inexperienced and poorly educated. Some carpetbaggers were thieves. In Louisiana, for example, one carpetbagger official was accused of stealing 100,000 dollars from state funds in his first year of office.

But Reconstruction governments also contained honest men who tried to improve the South. They passed laws to provide care for orphans and the blind, to encourage new industries and the building of railroads, and to build schools for both white and black children.

None of these improvements stopped southern whites from hating Reconstruction. This was not because of the incompetence or dishonesty of its governments. It was because Reconstruction aimed to give blacks the same rights that whites had. Southern whites were determined to prevent this. They organized terrorist groups to make white men the masters once more. The main aim of these groups was to threaten and frighten black people and prevent them from claiming their rights.

The largest and most feared terrorist group was a secret society called the Ku Klux Klan. Its members dressed themselves in white sheets and wore hoods to hide their faces. They rode by night through the southern countryside, beating and killing any blacks who tried to improve their position. Their sign was a burning wooden cross, which they placed outside the homes of their intended victims.

This use of violence and fear helped white racists to win back control of state governments all over the South. By 1876 Republican supporters of Reconstruction held power in only three southern

The Ku Klux Klan in 1915.

states. When Congress withdrew federal troops from the South in 1877, white Democrats won control of these, too. Reconstruction was over.

From this time onwards southern blacks were treated more and more as "second class citizens" – that is, they were not given equal treatment under the law. Most serious of all, they were robbed of their right to vote.

Some southern states prevented blacks from voting by saying that only people who paid a tax on voters – a poll tax – could do so. They then made the tax so high that most blacks could not afford to pay it. If blacks did try to pay, the tax collectors often refused to take their money. "Grandfather clauses" were also widely used to prevent blacks from voting. These clauses, or rules, allowed the vote only to people whose grandfathers had been qualified to vote in 1865. Most blacks had only obtained the vote in 1866 so the grandfather clauses automatically took away their voting rights.

The effects of grandfather clauses could be seen in the state of Louisiana. Before 1898 it had 164,088 white voters and 130,344 black voters. After Louisiana introduced a grandfather clause it still had 125,437 white voters, but only 5,320 black ones.

Once blacks lost the vote, taking away their other rights became easy. All the southern states passed laws to enforce strict racial separation, or "segregation." Segregation was enforced on trains, in parks, in schools, in restaurants, in theaters and swimming pools – even in cemeteries! Any black who dared to break these segregation laws was likely to end up either in prison or dead. In the 1890s an average of 150 blacks a year were killed illegally – "lynched" – by white mobs. It seemed that the improvements the Civil War and Reconstruction had brought black people were lost for ever.

But Reconstruction had not been for nothing. It had been the boldest attempt so far to achieve racial justice in the United States. The 14th Amendment was especially important. It was the foundation of the Civil Rights movement of the 1950s and 1960s and made it possible for Martin Luther King to cry out eventually on behalf of all black Americans:

"Free at last! Free at last! Thank God Almighty, we are free at last!"

Plessy v. *Ferguson*

In 1896 the Supreme Court announced its decision in a case called *Plessy* v. *Ferguson*. It ruled that the Constitution allowed separate facilities and services to be provided for black and white people, so long as the facilities and services were of equal quality. The *Plessy* v. *Ferguson* decision made racial segregation a legal part of the American way of life for more than half a century.

Southern states immediately began making separate but *unequal* provision for blacks. They passed laws to enforce segregation in every possible aspect of life – public transportation, theaters, hotels, eating places, parks, schools.

The "separate but equal" decision reached in *Plessy* v. *Ferguson* was at last overturned by another Supreme Court decision in 1954. In the case of *Brown* v. *Topeka*, the Supreme Court ruled that it was impossible for black children to receive an equal education in segregated schools. It ordered that all public schools in the United States should be opened to children of all races.

This 1954 decision to abandon *Plessy* v. *Ferguson* was a landmark in the black Civil Rights movement of the 1950s. It marked the beginning of a campaign to end all forms of legally enforced segregation in American life.

YEARS OF GROWTH

MINERS, RAILROADS AND CATTLEMEN

In March 1848, a group of workmen was building a sawmill beside a stream in California for a landowner named John Sutter. One day the foreman in charge of the workers saw golden specks glittering in the water. Picking up a handful of black gravel from the bed of the stream, he looked more closely. It was gold!

The foreman rushed to tell Sutter. Before long the news of his discovery was sweeping through California. By the middle of the summer a gold rush had begun. The governor of California reported to Washington that "mills are lying idle, fields of wheat are open to cattle and horses, houses vacant and farms going to waste" as men and women from all

Panning for gold in California.

over the territory hurried to the gold fields to make themselves rich.

By the spring of 1849, people from all over the world were rushing to California to look for gold. In 1848 its population was 15,000 people. By 1852 the population was more than 250,000. Some of the new arrivals traveled by sea to the port of San Francisco. Others traveled overland, enduring the same kind of hardships that faced settlers on the way to Oregon.

In the next twenty years gold discoveries attracted fortune-seekers to other parts of the far West. By the late 1850s they were mining in the mountains of Nevada and Colorado, by the 1860s they had moved into Montana and Wyoming and by the 1870s they were digging in the Black Hills of the Dakota country.

The first mining settlements were just untidy collections of tents and huts, scattered along rough tracks that were muddy in winter and dusty in summer. But some grew later into permanent communities. The present city of Denver, the capital of Colorado, began life in this way.

Thousands of miles separated these western mining settlements from the rest of the United States. Look at a map of the country at the end of the Civil War in 1865. You will see that white settlement in the East stops a little to the west of the Mississippi and Missouri rivers. Beyond these last farms, thousands of miles of flat or gently rolling land covered with tall grass stretched west to the foothills of the Rocky Mountains. Early travelers who passed through this region described it as a "sea of grass," for hardly any trees or bushes grew there. Geographers call these grasslands the Great Plains, or the Prairies, of North America.

The Great Plains are generally much drier than the lands to the east of the Mississippi. Rainfall ranges from about forty inches a year on the wetter, eastern edge, to less than eighteen inches a year in the western parts. Summer rain often pours down in fierce thunderstorms and can bring sudden and destructive floods. Droughts happen even more often than floods. These long, dry periods bring the danger of prairie fires, which race across the grasslands and burn everything in their path. In winter the Great Plains become very cold. Temperatures drop as low as −40° Fahrenheit and violent, windy snowstorms sweep across the flat, open land.

In the middle of the nineteenth century the Great Plains were the home of wandering Amerindian hunters such as the Sioux. The lives of these people depended upon the vast herds of buffalo that grazed on the sea of grass. The buffalo provided the Amerindians with everything they needed. They ate its meat. They made clothes from its skin. They also stretched its skin over poles to make the tepees they lived in. They shaped its bones into knives, tools, and ornaments.

In the 1840s and 1850s thousands of white people crossed the Great Plains to reach the farms of Oregon and the gold fields of California. To them the region was not somewhere to settle and make new homes but a place to pass through as quickly as possible. They saw it as unwelcoming and dangerous, and were happy to leave it to the Amerindians. They agreed with the mapmakers of the time, who wrote the name "Great American Desert" across the whole area.

Yet within twenty-five years of the end of the Civil War, practically all of the Great Plains had been divided into states and territories. Ranchers were feeding large herds of cattle on the "sea of grass," farmers were ploughing the "Great American Desert" to grow wheat, sheepherders were grazing their flocks on the foothills of the Rocky Mountains. By 1890 the separate areas of settlement on the Pacific Coast and along the Mississippi River had moved together. The frontier, that moving boundary of white settlement that had been one of the most important factors in American life ever since the time of the Pilgrims, had disappeared.

Railroads played an important part in this "closing" of the frontier. During the Civil War, Congress had become anxious to join the gold-rich settlements along the Pacific Coast more closely to the rest of the United States. In 1862 it granted land and money to

A poster advertising the opening of the railroad.

the Union Pacific Railroad Company to build a railroad west from the Mississippi towards the Pacific. At the same time it gave a similar grant to the Central Pacific Railroad Company to build eastwards from California.

Throughout the 1860s gangs of workmen labored with picks, shovels and gunpowder to build the two lines. Most of the workers on the Union Pacific were Irishmen or other recent immigrants from Europe. The Central Pacific workers were mainly Chinese, who had been brought to America under contract especially to do the job.

The railroad workers' progress depended mainly on the land over which they had to build. On the flat Great Plains they could move forward quickly, building up to six miles of railroad in a day. Among the rocks and cliffs of the Sierra Nevada mountains their progress was slower. Sometimes it would take days of difficult and dangerous tunneling to move forward a few yards.

The whole country watched with growing excitement as the two lines gradually approached one another. Both moved forward as fast as they could, for the grants of land and money that each company received from the government depended upon how many miles of railroad track it built. Finally, on May 10, 1869, the Central Pacific and the Union Pacific lines met at Promontory Point in Utah. A golden spike fixed the last rail into position. The first railroad across the North American continent was completed.

The new railroad was quickly joined by others. By 1884 four more major lines had crossed the continent to link the Mississippi valley with the Pacific Coast. These transcontinental railroads reduced the time that it took to travel across the United States from weeks to days.

As the railroads pushed west, cattle ranchers in Texas saw a way to make money. They could feed cattle cheaply on the grasslands between the Mississippi and the Rockies. Why not use the new railroads to transport the cattle to eastern cities where buyers were hungry for meat?

In the years after the Civil War, Texas cattle owners hired men called "drovers" or "cowboys" to drive their half-wild longhorn cattle north to the railroads. The cowboy's life was one of exhausting work, poor food and low pay. But to many young men it seemed free and exciting. Many cowboys were former Confederate soldiers who had moved west after the Civil War. Some were black ex-slaves from southern plantations. Others were boys from farms in the east who wanted a life with more adventure than farming could offer them.

The cattle traveled along regular routes called "trails." At the start of a trail drive the cowboys moved the herds quickly. But as they came closer to the railroad they slowed down, traveling only about twelve miles a day. This was to give the cattle plenty of time to graze, so that they would be as heavy as possible when they were sold.

New towns grew up where cattle trails met the railroads. The first of these "cattle towns" was Abilene, in Kansas. In 1867, cowboys drove 36,000 cattle there along the Chisholm Trail from Texas. As the railroad moved west, other cattle towns were built. The best known was Dodge City, which

The golden spike ceremony at Promontory Point, Utah, in 1869 marks the completion of the first transcontinental railroad.

reached the height of its fame between 1875 and 1885. In this period of ten years a quarter of a million Texas cattle traveled the trail to Dodge City. From there they went by rail to the slaughter houses of Chicago and Kansas City. Such cities grew rich from killing western cattle and preparing their meat for eating.

Very soon meat from the Great Plains was feeding people in Europe as well as the eastern United States. By 1881 more than 110 million pounds of American beef was being shipped across the Atlantic Ocean every year. The grass of the Great Plains was earning the United States as much money as the gold mines of its western mountains.

The Stampede *by Frederic Remington. A cowboy trying to control his herd of cattle which has been stampeded by lightning.*

On the trail

George Duffield was a cowboy. In 1866 he drove a herd of 1,000 Longhorn cattle north from Texas. The extracts below are from his diary:

May 8
Rain pouring down in torrents. Ran my horse into a ditch and got my knee badly sprained.

May 14
Brazos River. Swam our cattle and horses and built raft and rafted our provisions and blankets and so on over. Swam river with rope and then hauled wagon over. Lost most of our kitchen furniture, such as camp kettles, coffee pot, cups, etc.

June 1
Stampede last night and a general mix up and loss of beeves [cattle]. Hunt cattle again. Men all tired and want to leave.

June 2
Hard rain and wind storm. Beeves ran and I had to be on horseback all night. Awful night. Men lost. Quit the beeves and go hunting men. Found our men with Indian guide and 195 beeves 14 miles from camp. Almost starved not having had a bite to eat for 60 hours. Got to camp about 12:00. Tired.

June 19
Arkansas River. 15 Indians came to herd and tried to take some beeves. Would not let them. One drew his knife and I my revolver. Made them leave, but fear they have gone for others.

61

—— 15 ——

FARMING THE GREAT PLAINS

In 1862 Union and Confederate armies were fighting some of the bloodiest battles of the Civil War. But that same year Congress found time to pass a law that had nothing to do with the war. The law was called the Homestead Act.

The Homestead Act offered free farms ("homesteads") in the West to families of settlers. Each homestead consisted of 160 acres of land and any head of a family who was at least twenty-one years of age and an American citizen could claim one. So could immigrants who intended to become citizens. All that homesteaders had to do was to move onto a piece of public land – that is, land owned by the government – live on it for five years and the land became theirs. If a family wanted to own its homestead more quickly than this it could buy the land after only six months for a very low price of $1.25 an acre.

A railroad company poster advertising land for settlers.

Transcontinental railroad companies like the Union Pacific also provided settlers with cheap land. These companies had been given land beside their tracks by the government. To increase their profits they were keen for people to begin farming this land so they advertised for settlers. They did this not only in the eastern United States, but as far away as Europe. They shipped immigrants across the Atlantic, gave them free railroad transport to the West and often helped them to start their farms and communities.

East of the Mississippi, small family farms were the usual way of cultivating the land. From the 1870s onwards farms of this sort began to spread over the Great Plains. As a boy, Hamlin Garland was taken to live on the Plains by his parents. Years later he remembered the first sight of the land that was to be his new home:

"Each mile took us farther and farther into the unsettled prairie until in the afternoon of the second day, we came to a meadow so wide that its western rim touched the sky . . . The plain was covered with grass as tall as ripe wheat and when my father stopped his team [of horses, pulling the wagon] and came back to us and said, 'Well, children, here we are on The Big Prairie', we looked around us with awe."

Building a house was the first task the homesteaders faced. They had to do this themselves, for there was no one else to do it for them. But they had a problem. What could they use as building material? No trees grew on the plains, only mile after mile of long, waving grass.

The settlers built their houses from the matted roots of this grass. They cut thick pieces of earth and grass roots – "sods" – from the dry ground and used them as building bricks. This custom earned homesteaders a nickname by which they were often known – "sod busters."

These same tangled grass roots also gave homesteaders a lot of trouble. The Great Plains had never before been ploughed. The roots of its grasses formed a tangled mat at least four inches thick. When farmers tried to cut through this mat to sow their

A settlement beside the transcontinental railroad.

seeds it often broke or twisted the iron blades of their ploughs.

Lack of water was another problem. The Great Plains had few streams and the rainfall was so low and unreliable that farmers often watched their crops shrivel up and die in the dry ground. Fire was another danger of the long, dry summers. A lightning flash, or even a small spark, could start a fire that would race across the prairie faster than a horse could gallop.

In some years plagues of insects caused even more destruction than fire. Between 1874 and 1877 grasshoppers swarmed across the plains in millions, eating everything they found – crops, leather boots, clothing, wooden door frames. In one place they stopped a railroad engine by covering the track until the rails became too slippery for the engine to move.

Some homesteaders were discouraged by such problems. They gave up their land and moved back east. But most stayed. Gradually they began to overcome their early difficulties. Ploughs with steel blades enabled them to cut through the prairie sod and cultivate the soil beneath. Mechanical reapers made it possible to harvest wheat crops ten times faster than before. Pumps driven by the prairie winds raised life-giving water from hundreds of feet below the dry surface of the land. Barbed wire fences stopped straying cattle from trampling crops into the ground.

None of these aids were made by the farmers themselves. They were manufactured in big new factories in cities like Chicago. From Chicago the railroads carried them out to the Plains. The railroads

Homesteaders and cattlemen

The first homesteaders often quarrelled with cattlemen. The different ways in which the two groups used the land made trouble between them almost certain. Cattle ranchers and cowboys complained that homesteaders were blocking the cattle trails and said that their ploughed fields were a waste of good grazing land. Homesteaders became angry when their crops were eaten or trampled upon by the ranchers' cattle. They began to build barbed wire fences around their land to stop this. This made the cattlemen even more angry, especially if the land that was fenced off included a stream that their cattle depended upon for drinking water. One cowboy put the cattleman's point of view in these words:

"Those jayhawkers [thieves] would take up a claim right where the herds watered and charge us for water. They would plant a crop alongside the trail and plow a furrow around it for a fence, and then when the cattle got into their wheat or their garden patch, they would come out cussing [cursing] and waving a shotgun and yelling for damages. And the cattle had been coming through there when they were still growing pumpkins [vegetables] in Illinois."

In some places people were killed in "range wars" as both cattlemen and homesteaders used guns to protect their interests. It took years for the two groups to learn to live peacefully side by side.

The Fall of the Cowboy *by Frederic Remington. The invention of barbed wire and the fencing of the prairies threatened the life of the cowboy.*

Joseph Glidden's barbed wire

In 1874 an Illinois farmer named Joseph Glidden patented an invention. He advertised it as "stronger than whiskey and cheaper than air." His invention provided prairie farmers with something that, in a land without trees, they desperately needed – a cheap and efficient fencing material. Glidden's invention was barbed wire.

Barbed wire consists of two strands of plain wire twisted around one another, with short, sharp wire spikes held between them. By 1890, 100 pounds of barbed wire was being sold for only $4. Prairie farmers bought tons of it to fence in their lands.

Barbed wire fences meant that prairie farmers could plant crops knowing that straying cattle would not trample and eat the growing plants. They could breed better animals knowing that stray bulls could not mate with their cows. They could mark off their boundaries to avoid quarrels with neighbors.

Glidden's invention changed the face of the Great Plains. By the end of the century thousands of miles of barbed wire fences had divided the open prairie into a patchwork of separate farms and fields.

also carried away the farmers' crops. This made it possible for the farmers to sell their produce in far-away places. Before the end of the nineteenth century wheat grown on the Great Plains of North America was feeding millions of people, not only in the United States but thousands of miles away in Europe.

But prairie farmers still had problems. The Homestead Act gave them land, but it failed to give them a sure living. On the well-watered lands east of the Mississippi a farmer could easily support a family on a homestead of 160 acres. On the rain-starved Great Plains no farmer could make a living from a farm of that size. His crops of wheat were too small; his animals were too hungry.

Prairie farmers worked hard to survive. They ploughed up and planted more land. But if the rains failed, the sun burned up their crops and the prairie winds blew away their dusty top soil, leaving the land poorer and less productive. Even when enough rain fell for the crops to grow well, farmers could still be in trouble. In such years the land produced so much wheat that the prices for which individual farmers were able to sell it were too low to give them a decent living.

In the last thirty years of the nineteenth century such "over-production" became a big problem for American farmers. Its cause was not only that farmers were cultivating more land. Improved agricultural machines were also making their farms more productive every year. "Gang" ploughs with several blades made it possible to prepare more land for sowing more quickly. Giant machines called "combine harvesters" cut and threshed wheat in one operation.

Farmers formed political action groups to try to improve their position. The groups were particularly keen to force railroad companies to reduce the high prices that they charged to transport farmers' crops. They included the Patrons of Husbandry, which was formed in the 1870s, and the Populist Party of the 1890s. Members of the Patrons of Husbandry were also known as "Grangers." The voting power of the Grangers caused many western states to pass "Granger laws." These laws set up government bodies to control railroad freight charges and to look after farmers' interests in other matters.

Grangers also joined together in cooperative societies. Some of these cooperatives failed because the farmers who ran them lacked business experience. Others survive even today. In many western farming communities cooperative organizations still compete with privately owned firms both to supply the farmer's needs and to buy his produce.

John Muir and the national parks

For hundreds of years land, water, trees and wild animals were so plentiful in America that people thought they would never run out. It became a habit with Americans to use natural resources carelessly and wastefully.

As settlers spread across America, all of them – farmers, miners, ranchers, lumberjacks – robbed the land and destroyed its resources. Trees were felled in millions. Rivers and lakes were choked by waste from mines and factories. Vast buffalo herds were almost entirely destroyed, as were many other wild animals, including wolves, sea otters and fur seals.

Naturalists were alarmed by this destruction. They demanded that the government and people of the United States should conserve (save) the nation's natural heritage. One of the leaders of these "conservationists" was John Muir. Muir, who had been born in Scotland, traveled about the American West studying and describing its natural wonders. He worked hard to persuade people to protect these wonders for the benefit of future generations.

Largely because of Muir's efforts, big areas of unspoiled land were made into public parks. One of these was Yosemite Park in California. The heart of Yosemite is a beautiful valley surrounded by cliffs and mountain peaks. Giant Sequoia trees and other rare plants grow there. In 1890 Yosemite became a national park – that is, a park belonging to the whole nation.

Yosemite was not the United States' first national park. That was Yellowstone Park. This is a 3,458 square-mile area of volcanic rocks and forest in the Rocky Mountains and it became a national park in 1872.

Yellowstone is one of the world's largest wildlife sanctuaries. Bears, mountain sheep, buffalo, moose and more than two hundred kinds of birds make their homes there. Its most famous sight, however, is "Old Faithful." This is a volcanic geyser which every hour shoots approximately 10,000 gallons of water almost 165 feet into the air.

When Theodore Roosevelt became President in 1901 he set up more big national parks and forests. In 1916 Congress established the National Parks Service to look after them. The American system of national parks became one of the most admired in the world. It has been taken as an example by many other countries.

Yellowstone National Park.

THE AMERINDIANS' LAST STAND

What happened to the Amerindians as white people spread across the plains and mountains of the American West? This chapter aims to answer that question.

When the cowboys and homesteaders arrived on the Great Plains, Amerindian peoples like the Sioux had been roaming across them for hundreds of years. The Sioux lived by hunting the buffalo. In the early part of the nineteenth century an estimated twelve million of these gentle, heavy animals wandered the Great Plains. They moved about in herds. Sometimes these herds were so big that they stretched as far as the eye could see. The buffalo provided the Sioux with everything that they needed – food, clothing, tools, homes.

In the 1840s wagon trains heading for Oregon and California began to cross the Great Plains. The Amerindians usually let them pass without trouble. Then railroads began to push across the grasslands. The railroads carried white people who stayed on the prairies and began to plough them.

At first the Amerindians tried to drive the newcomers away from their hunting grounds. But soon they saw that this was impossible. So they made treaties with the government in Washington, giving up large pieces of their land for white farmers to settle upon. In 1851 the Pawnee people signed away an area that today forms most of the state of Nebraska. In 1858 the Sioux gave up an area almost as big in South Dakota. In the 1860s the Comanche and the Kiowa gave up lands in Kansas, Colorado and Texas. In return for such agreements the government promised to leave the Amerindians in peace on the lands that remained theirs.

The Fort Laramie treaty of 1868 was typical of these agreements. So was what happened to it. In this treaty the government declared that large areas between the Missouri River and the Rocky Mountains belonged to the Sioux. It gave a solemn promise that the lands would remain Sioux property "as long as the grass should grow and the water flow."

Fine and moving words. Six years later, however, American soldiers found gold in the Black Hills of South Dakota. The Black Hills were sacred to the Sioux and when the government tried to buy them, the Sioux refused to sell. "One does not sell the Earth upon which the people walk," said a chief named Crazy Horse. But the American government ignored the Sioux's refusal. It broke the Fort Laramie treaty and allowed prospectors and miners to enter the Black Hills. In the winter of 1875 thousands of white men poured into the area.

By this time the Amerindian peoples of the Great Plains were facing another serious problem. The buffalo was beginning to disappear. More and more of the land that the big animals needed to graze upon was being taken by ranchers and farmers. Worse still, white hunters were shooting down the buffalo in thousands. They killed them for their hides or for sport and left their flesh to rot. In just two years between 1872 and 1874 the hunters almost completely destroyed the great herds. A visitor to the Plains in 1873 described what he saw there. "Where there were myriads [vast numbers] of buffalo the year before, there were now myriads of corpses."

The Amerindians could not understand this behavior. "Has the white man become a child that he should recklessly kill and not eat?" asked a Kiowa chief. But the American army encouraged the slaughter. General Sheridan, the officer who commanded the army in the West, saw the extermination of the buffalo as a way to end Amerindian resistance to the occupation of their land. "These men [the buffalo hunters] have done more in the last two years to settle the Indian question than the entire regular army has done in the last thirty years," he wrote. "Send them powder and lead and for the sake of lasting peace let them kill, skin, and sell until the buffaloes are exterminated."

As more settlers claimed homesteads in the West the American government needed more land for them. To obtain this it decided to force the Amerindians to give up their wandering way of life. It sent soldiers to

Custer's Last Stand.

drive the Amerindians onto "reservations." These reservations were areas of land that were usually so dry or rocky that the government thought white settlers were never likely to want them.

The Amerindians fought back. One of their best known leaders was Sitting Bull of the Sioux. "We lived in our country in the way our fathers and our fathers' fathers lived before us and we sought trouble with no men," he said later. "But the soldiers came into our country and fired upon us and we fought back. Is it so bad to fight in defense of one's country and loved ones?"

The Amerindians were outnumbered and outgunned. But they inflicted some surprising defeats on the American soldiers. They won their best known victory at the Battle of the Little Big Horn in June 1876. On a hill beside the Little Big Horn River 3,000 Sioux and Cheyenne warriors led by Crazy Horse surrounded and killed all 225 men of a company of United States cavalry. The dead included the cavalrymen's commander, General George Armstrong Custer. For this reason the battle is sometimes called "Custer's Last Stand."

The Battle of the Little Big Horn was also the last stand for the Amerindians. The American government and people were angry at the defeat of their soldiers. They felt that they had been humiliated. More soldiers were sent west to hunt down Custer's killers. The Sioux were too weak to fight back. With the buffalo gone, more of their people were dying every day of starvation and disease. The Sioux surrendered and the soldiers marched them away to the reservations.

Other Amerindians were no more fortunate than the Sioux. By 1890 most of the American West, from the Mississippi River to the Pacific Ocean, was occupied by cattle ranchers, farmers, or miners. The Amerindians had nothing left except the reservations.

The United States government said that it would help and protect the reservation Amerindians. It

Ghost Dancers.

promised them food, materials to build homes, tools to cultivate the land. But the promises were often broken. There was great suffering on the reservations. Epidemic diseases swept through them, killing their people.

In 1890 a religious prophet told the Sioux to dance a special dance called the Ghost Dance. He told them that if they did so a great miracle would take place. Their dead warriors would come back to life, the buffalo would return and all the white men would be swept away by a great flood.

The Ghost Dance movement was peaceful. But the Dancers' beliefs worried the government. So did the fact that some of them waved rifles above their heads as they danced. It ordered the army to arrest the movement's leaders.

On a cold December day in 1890 a group of 350 Sioux, 120 men and 230 women and children, left their reservation. Led by a chief named Big Foot, they set off to join another group nearby for safety. But a party of soldiers stopped them on the way and marched them to an army post at Wounded Knee Creek.

The Ghost Dancers' Song

Father, have pity on us
We are crying for thirst
All is gone!
We have nothing to eat
Father, we are poor.
We are very poor.
The buffalo are gone.
They are all gone.
Take pity on us, Father,
We are dancing as you wished
Because you commanded us.
We dance hard, we dance long –
Have pity,
Father, help us
You are close by in the dark
Hear us and help us.
Take away the white men
Send back the buffalo
We are poor and weak
We can do nothing alone
Help us to be what we once were –
Happy hunters of buffalo.

The frozen body of Big Foot at Wounded Knee.

Next morning the soldiers ordered the Sioux to give up their guns. One young warrior refused. A shot rang out, followed by many more. The soldiers began shooting down the Sioux women and children as well as the men. Within minutes most of the Sioux were dead or badly wounded. Many of the wounded who crawled away died later in a blizzard that swept over the camp.

At the time Americans called what happened at Wounded Knee a battle. Other people since have called it a massacre. But whatever the events at Wounded Knee are called, one thing is certain. For the Sioux they marked the end of all hope of a return to their old way of life.

But the Sioux, like other Amerindians, survived. In 1924 Congress passed the Indian Citizenship Act. This recognized Amerindians as full citizens of the United States and gave them the right to vote. In 1934 the Indian Reorganization Act encouraged them to set up their own councils to run the affairs of their reservations.

In spite of such improvements, Amerindians remained far behind most other Americans in health, wealth, and education. Look at some facts from the 1980s. The unemployment rate among Amerindians was 39 percent, more than five times the figure for the population as a whole. Almost 25 percent of Amerindian families were living on incomes too low to buy the food, clothing, and housing they needed to keep in good health. Diseases like diabetes, pneumonia, influenza, and alcohol addiction were killing twice as many Amerindians as other Americans.

In the 1970s Amerindians from all over the United States joined together to try to improve their position. They formed the American Indian Movement and in 1972 thousands of them traveled to Washington to take part in a protest march that they called the "Trail of Broken Treaties." The next year a group armed with rifles occupied the small South Dakota village that now stands on the site of the Battle of Wounded Knee. They stayed there for seventy-one days. Their aim was to draw attention to their demand for the return of lands unjustly taken away from their ancestors.

Amerindian militants at Wounded Knee.

Other Amerindians sued the United States government in court for breaking the old treaties. The Sioux, for example, demanded the return of the Black Hills. The courts decided in their favor and awarded them $122.5 million in compensation for the loss of their land. Many Sioux did not want to accept the money, however. They continued to demand the return of the sacred land itself.

When he was a very old man, a survivor of the Battle of Wounded Knee named Black Elk said goodbye to the old way of life of his people with these words:

"I did not know then how much was ended. When I look back now from this high hill of my old age, I can still see the butchered women and children lying heaped and scattered all along the crooked gulch as plain as when I saw them with eyes still young. And I can see that something else died there in the bloody mud, and was buried in the blizzard. A people's dream died there. It was a beautiful dream."

Amerindians today have different dreams. But they have not forgotten the old ones. Let the college-educated great-grandson of a famous Apache warrior have the last word:

"My generation spent all their time learning the white man's ways. We mastered them but we lost a lot of our Indian heritage. Now we are trying to regain what we lost."

The story of Sitting Bull

In the year 1831 a baby boy was born in a tepee village on the Dakota grasslands. His parents were Sioux and they named him Sitting Bull.

Sitting Bull grew up to be a respected leader of his people. He did not take part in the fighting at the 1876 Battle of the Little Big Horn. But after the battle he defended the actions of his people:

"We were camped there awaiting the will of the Great Spirit, praying to the Great Spirit to save us from the hands of our enemies, now near and coming to complete our extermination. My men destroyed them in a very short time. Now they accuse me of slaying them. Yet what did I do? Nothing. We did not go out of our country to kill them. They came to kill us and got killed themselves. The Great Spirit so ordered it."

After their victory at the Little Big Horn the Amerindians were pursued by the army. In 1877 Sitting Bull led some of his followers to safety across the border in Canada, but in 1881 he returned to the United States. His clothes were in rags and he looked old and defeated. But as he handed over his rifle to the American soldiers he told them proudly, "I wish it to be remembered that I was the last man of my tribe to surrender my rifle."

Sitting Bull continued to fight for the rights of his people in other ways. He criticized the American government for neglecting and cheating the Amerindians on the reservations. "It is your doing that we are here," he told a group of visiting Congressmen. "You sent us here and told us to live as you do." He told them that if the government wanted the Amerindians to become like white men then it must supply them with tools, animals and wagons "because that is the way white people make a living."

In 1885 the famous showman Buffalo Bill Cody offered Sitting Bull a job. He wanted the old leader to become one of the attractions of his traveling Wild West Show. The reservation authorities were glad to be rid of Sitting Bull and

Sitting Bull.

quickly gave him permission to go. The following year Cody again asked Sitting Bull to join him, this time on a tour of Europe. Sitting Bull refused. "I am needed here," he told Cody. "There is more talk of taking our lands."

When the Ghost Dance movement began the government accused Sitting Bull of being its leader. In December 1890, it sent armed policemen to arrest him. As Sitting Bull stepped out of the door of his cabin on the reservation one of the policemen shot him dead. The killer was a Sioux, one of Sitting Bull's own people.

INVENTORS AND INDUSTRIES

In 1876 President Ulysses S. Grant traveled to Philadelphia to open a special exhibition. The exhibition was called the Centennial Exposition. It had been organized to celebrate the United States' hundredth birthday as an independent nation by showing some of its achievements.

The main attraction of the Centennial Exposition was the Machinery Hall. This was a big wooden building that covered more than twelve acres. Inside it visitors could see such recent American inventions as the typewriter and the telephone as well as machines for countless other uses – for sewing, grinding, screwing, printing, drilling, pumping, hammering.

President Grant and Emperor Dom Pedro II of Brazil start the Corliss Centennial Engine in Machinery Hall.

In the six months that the Exposition was open almost ten million people wandered through the hall. They gazed in wonder at its hundreds of machines. Even the normally patronizing British newspaper *The Times* was impressed. "The American invents as the Greek sculpted and as the Italian painted," it reported. "It is genius."

At the time of the Centennial Exposition, the United States was still mainly a farming country. But in the years that followed, American industries grew quickly. The production of coal and iron grew especially fast. These were the most important industrial raw materials in the nineteenth century.

Americans discovered vast new deposits of both in the 1880s and 1890s. In a range of low hills at the western end of Lake Superior, for example, some brothers named Merritt found the great Mesabi iron deposits. The Merritts made their discovery in 1887 and the Mesabi soon became one of the largest producers of iron ore in the world. The ore lay close to the surface of the ground in horizontal bands up to 500 feet thick. It was cheap, easy to mine, and remarkably free of chemical impurities. Before long Mesabi ore was being processed into high quality steel at only one tenth of the previous cost.

By 1900 ten times more coal was being produced in the United States than in 1860. The output of iron was twenty times higher. These increases were both a cause and a result of a rapid growth of American manufacturing industries in these years.

Railroads were very important in this growth of manufacturing. Vast amounts of coal and iron were used to make steel for their rails, locomotives, freight wagons and passenger cars. But this was not all. The railroads linked together buyers and sellers all over the country. Without them big new centers of industry like Pittsburgh and Chicago could not have developed. It was the railroads that carried cattle to Chicago from the Great Plains to keep its huge slaughter houses and meat processing plants busy. It was the railroads, too, that took reapers, windmills and barbed wire from Chicago's farm equipment factories to homesteaders on the prairies.

Thomas Edison

Americans have always been proud of their ability to find practical solutions to practical problems. During the nineteenth century they developed thousands of products to make life easier, safer or more enjoyable for people. Barbed wire is one example, the sewing machine is another.

Up to the middle of the nineteenth century the inventors of such products often had little scientific knowledge. Their inventions were based on practical "know-how." So long as the inventions worked, everyone was satisfied.

Many later developments, however, called for an understanding of basic scientific principles in, for example, electricity, magnetism and chemistry. One man above all others showed an ability to use such knowledge to solve everyday problems. His name was Thomas Alva Edison.

Edison was born in 1847 and died in 1931. He made more than a thousand original inventions. Edison's laboratory contained every material and chemical that was then known. Wearing a long, white chemist's coat, his fingers stained by chemicals and his hair dirty with oil and dust, he would work for days without eating or sleeping when he was close to solving a problem.

Some of Edison's sayings became almost as well known as his inventions. "There is no substitute for hard work" was one of them. Sometimes he took this principle too far. On the day he got married, for example, he forgot his bride and spent the night working in his laboratory.

Edison had his greatest success in making practical use of electricity. In 1878 he formed the Edison Electric Light Company. He had a clear commercial aim – to capture from gas the huge market for lighting homes, streets and places of work.

Thomas Edison in his laboratory.

To do this, one thing Edison had to develop was a long-lasting, glowing electric light bulb. The problem was to find a suitable material for the filament of the bulb. What was needed was a filament that would glow brightly when the current of electricity passed through it, but without burning out. Edison tried platinum, paper, leather, wood, cotton. Some glowed for minutes, some for hours, but none for long enough to satisfy him. Then he found the answer – bamboo! When he gave a public demonstration of his light bulb the value of shares in the Edison Electric Light Company rose from $100 to $3,000 each.

Edison then built complete electrical generating systems to provide his bulbs with power. He developed dynamos to produce the electricity, underground cables to carry it to where it was needed, fuse boxes to make it safe to use.

The Age of Electricity had begun. Soon electricity would not only light streets, but heat houses, power machines, drive railroad engines. It would become what it has remained ever since – the world's chief source of energy.

By 1890 the industries of the United States were earning the country more than its farmlands. In the twenty years that followed, industrial output went on growing, faster and faster. By 1913 more than one third of the whole world's industrial production was pouring from the mines and factories of the United States.

The growth of American industry was organized and controlled by businessmen who found the money to pay for it. Many of these men began their lives in poverty. By a mixture of hard work and ability, and by ignoring the rights of others, they made themselves wealthy and powerful. Their admirers

Steel being forged at Carnegie's Pennsylvania Iron and Steel Works.

called such men "captains of industry." Their critics called them "robber barons" – or worse!

Andrew Carnegie was one of the best known of these men. Carnegie was born in Scotland in 1835, but immigrated to America at the age of thirteen. He began his life there working for one dollar twenty cents a week in a Pittsburgh cotton mill. From there he moved to a job in a telegraph office, then to one on the Pennsylvania Railroad. By the time he was thirty he already had an income of over forty thousand dollars a year from far-sighted investments.

Carnegie concentrated his investments in the iron and steel business. By the 1860s he controlled companies making bridges, rails, and locomotives for the railroads. In the 1870s he built the biggest steel mill in America on the Monongahela River in Pennsylvania. He also bought coal and iron ore mines, a fleet of steamships to carry ore across the Great Lakes from Mesabi to a port he owned on Lake Erie, and a railroad to connect the port to his steel works in Pennsylvania.

Nothing like Carnegie's wealth and industrial power had ever before been seen in America. By 1900, as owner of half the shares in the giant Carnegie Steel Corporation, his annual income was estimated to be over twenty-three million dollars – this was about twenty thousand times more than the income of the average American of the day.

The great wealth of men like Carnegie came partly from their success in swallowing up rival firms or driving them out of business. Businessmen like Carnegie and John D. Rockefeller, the "king" of the growing oil industry, realized that they could greatly increase their profits by doing this. They could reduce the costs of running their companies, and with no competitors to challenge their position they could raise the prices of their products to whatever level they wished.

Eli Whitney and the American system

Eli Whitney, the man who invented the cotton gin, never made much money from it. Too many people copied his original machine without paying him anything.

In about 1800 Whitney began to make guns. Until this time these had always been made by skilled gunmakers. Each gun was individually made, entirely by one man and a part from one gun would not necessarily fit another. Whitney changed this. At a factory he opened in Newhaven, Connecticut, he began to use machines to make guns. His machines made individual parts for guns in separate operations and in large numbers. Most important of all, they made parts that were exactly alike, so that any part would fit any gun. This made it possible for guns to be put together in stages, with different workers each carrying out one particular task.

Whitney's way of working meant that guns could now be made by men without enough skill to make a complete gun. He had worked out the main ideas of a way of manufacturing that would later become known as the "American system." Later still this American system became known as "mass production." Mass production was a very important discovery. Without it the standard of living of today's United States, and that of the entire industrialized world, would not be possible.

Henry Ford and mass production

Henry Ford is famous for making automobiles. But what makes him important is *how* he made them.

Ford began to make automobiles in the 1890s. One day in 1903 he was talking to a friend about the best way to do this. "The real way is to make one like another, as much alike as pins or matches," he said. The friend said that he did not believe that this was possible. "The principle is just the same," Ford replied. "All you need is more space."

Ford tried out his idea with an automobile called the Model T. Like Whitney's guns, every Model T was put together or "assembled" from exactly the same parts. The cars were even painted the same color. "A customer can have an automobile painted any color that he wants," Ford is supposed to have said, "so long as it is black."

This use of identical parts in manufacturing is called "standardization." Ford added to it the idea of a moving assembly line. The idea of the assembly line is to save time. It does this by positioning workers in a factory in one place and taking work to them.

Ford first used an assembly line to make magnetos for his Model Ts. By the old method one man on his own did this job from start to finish. Ford divided the work into twenty-one separate actions. A different man carried out each one as the magneto moved past him on a moving belt called a "conveyor." The change reduced the time taken to put together a magneto from twenty minutes to five.

In 1913 Ford started to use assembly-line methods to make the complete Model T. As the cars moved along on a conveyor, dozens of workmen each carried out a single operation – tightening certain nuts or fixing certain parts. By the time a car reached the end of the line it was complete. It was filled up with gasoline and driven off ready for the road. Making a car in this new way took 1 hour and 33 minutes. Making one previously had taken 12 hours and 28 minutes.

By combining standardization and the assembly line Ford showed manufacturers of all kinds how to produce goods cheaply and in large quantities. Because of this he is seen as the father of twentieth-century mass production.

The giant industrial organizations that such men created were known as "corporations." As they grew bigger and more powerful still, they often became "trusts." By the early twentieth century trusts controlled large parts of American industry. One trust controlled the steel industry, another the oil industry, another the meat-packing industry, and there were many more. The biggest trusts were richer than most nations. By their wealth and power – and especially their power to decide wages and prices – they controlled the lives of millions of people.

Many Americans were alarmed by the power of the trusts. The United States was a land that was supposed to offer equal opportunities to everyone. Yet now it seemed that the country was coming under the control of a handful of rich and powerful men who were able to do more or less anything they wished. Some bribed politicians to pass laws which favored them. Others hired private armies to crush any attempt by their workers to obtain better conditions. Their attitude to the rights of other people was summed up in a famous remark of the railroad "king" William H. Vanderbilt. Vanderbilt was asked whether he thought that railroads should be run in the public interest. "The public be damned!" he replied.

The contemptuous way in which leaders of industry like Vanderbilt rejected criticism made people angry. It strengthened the feeling that something ought to be done to limit such men's growing power over the nation's life. Many people came to see this matter as the most important problem facing the United States in the early years of the twentieth century. Unless something was done about it, they feared, the United States would become a nation whose life was controlled by a handful of rich businessmen.

18

THE GOLDEN DOOR

The unveiling of the Statue of Liberty.

On a small island in New York harbor stands a giant statue of a robed woman. She looks out to sea, her right arm holding a torch high in the air. She is the Statue of Liberty, one of the best-known landmarks in the world. The Statue of Liberty was presented to the United States in 1886. It was given by the people of France to mark the hundredth anniversary of the War of Independence.

For millions of immigrants the Statue of Liberty has been their first sight of America. Carved on its base are words that for more than a hundred years now have offered them hope:

> Give me your tired, your poor,
> Your huddled masses yearning to breathe free
> The wretched refuse of your teeming shore
> Send these, the homeless tempest-tossed to me,
> I lift my lamp beside the golden door.

The story of the American people is a story of immigrants. More than 75 percent of all the people in history who have ever left their homelands to live in another country have moved to the United States. In the course of its history it has taken in more people from other lands than any other country in the world. Since the founding of Jamestown in 1607 more than fifty million people from other lands have made new homes there.

Between 1840 and 1860 more immigrants than ever before arrived. Most came from Europe. Poor crops, hunger and political unrest caused an estimated five million Europeans a year to leave the lands of their birth at this time. More of them went to the United States than to any other country.

Among these immigrants were many Irish people. The Irish depended for food upon their crops of potatoes. For five years after 1845 these became diseased and rotted in the fields. About 750,000 Irish people starved to death. Many of the survivors left Ireland and went to the United States. In 1847 alone more than 118,000 of them immigrated there. By 1860 one in every four of the people living in the city of New York had been born in Ireland. Today more than thirteen million Americans have Irish ancestors.

During the Civil War in the 1860s the federal government encouraged more emigration from Europe. It did this by offering land to immigrants who would serve as soldiers in the Union armies. By 1865 about one in five of the soldiers in the armies of the North was a wartime immigrant. Many had come from Germany. Today about one in three of all Americans have German ancestors.

Ireland is in the west of Europe. Germany is in the north. Until about 1880 most immigrants to the United States came from these regions. Then a big change took place. More emigrants from lands in the south and east of Europe began to arrive – Italians, Poles, Greeks, Russians, Hungarians, Czechs. By 1896 more than half of all the immigrants entering the United States were from eastern or southern Europe.

Immigrants sailing to America.

grow up as Americans. Because of that he could never feel bitter . . .''

Between 1880 and 1925 about two million Jews entered the United States. Today there are about 5.7 million Jewish Americans and they make up about 2.2 percent of the total population of the United States. In certain states along the Atlantic coast the percentage of Jews is higher. In the state of New York, for example, one person in ten is Jewish.

So many immigrants wanted to enter the United States in the late 1800s that the government found it difficult to keep check on them. To control the situation it opened a special place of entry in New York harbor. This place was called Ellis Island. All intending immigrants were examined there before they were allowed to enter the United States.

Ellis Island was opened in 1892. During its busiest times it dealt with almost 2,000 immigrants a day. Between its opening and 1954, when it closed its

Many Jewish people came to the United States at this time. In the 1880s Jews were being killed all over eastern Europe in bloody massacres called "pogroms." Many thousands escaped by leaving for the United States. Leon Stein was the son of one of them. Many years later he explained why his father, despite the hardship that he suffered in America, had wanted to live there:

"... the exploitation of labor was fearful and my father was having a terrible time. He was just getting by, making a living working twelve to fourteen hours a day. And he was suffering like a coal miner suffers, because in the sweat-shops [clothing factories], at that time, instead of coal dust what you got was lint ... Lint got down the throat and into the lungs and caused the same coughing, the same diseases, the same sickness as dust. And in the end it killed you. And in the end it probably was what killed him ...

But he still wanted to live in America. He never became rich, he never became successful – and he never became bitter ... Remember, he had come from a place where, if you were Jewish, you didn't count as a human being and you had no rights at all. In America they gave my father the vote, they allowed him a place to live, and they let his children

Leaving home

Leon Stein's mother was born in a small village in Lithuania. At the age of eighty-six she still remembered vividly the day in 1908 that she left her village and set off for America as an immigrant:

"I remember it clearly. The whole village turned out to wave us goodby and we were all sitting in the cart with our little bundles on our laps and our shawls around our shoulders. I was excited a little bit, but mostly rather miserable and frightened. As the cart got to the end of the village street I could see the group of villagers who were waving us goodby was getting smaller and smaller, but I kept my eyes fixed on my mother in the front of that little group. I didn't take my eyes off her ... Then, just before the cart turned the corner and I lost sight of them, I saw my mother faint and fall to the ground crying and weeping, and I saw the rest of the group bend over her to pick her up, and I tried to get out of the cart and run back to her and stay with her. But the others with me in the cart stopped me and held onto me. And the cart turned the corner. And I was weeping and struggling and they were holding me. And I never saw my mother again."

Immigrant children being examined by a health officer at Ellis Island.

doors, more than twenty million people waited anxiously in its halls and corridors. Immigration officers asked these people questions to find out if they were criminals or mentally abnormal. Doctors examined them for disease. A letter chalked on their clothing – H for heart disease or E for eye disease – could end their hopes of a new life in America.

But most passed the examinations. Almost half of all present-day Americans have ancestors who entered the United States by way of Ellis Island. Listen to Leon Stein again. One day in the 1970s he stood in Ellis Island's echoing, empty Great Hall and spoke quietly of the way that it made him feel:

"My parents came through this place at the turn of the century. How can I stand here and not be moved? I feel it is haunted. I think if you become really quiet you can actually hear all the crying, all the feeling, all the impatience, all the misunderstanding that went on in this hall. Being born again is not an easy thing and the people who came through here were being born again. This was their gateway to hope, to a new life."

The immigrants found work in busy cities like New York, Chicago and Pittsburgh – stitching garments, feeding furnaces, laboring on factory assembly lines, hacking out coal. They worked hard because they wanted to make a success of their new life. Yet for

most immigrants this new life was a hard one. They were outsiders in a strange land. Often they could not even speak its language. Only the hardest and lowest paid jobs were open to them. Like Leon Stein's father, they had to work for long hours in dangerous conditions and to live in overcrowded slums that were breeding places of disease and misery.

Yet bad as conditions were, they often seemed preferable to those the immigrants had left behind in Europe. In the United States they were free from religious and political persecution. They were often better dressed and better fed than they had ever been before. They marveled at such wonders as free schools for their children, at the lamps glowing along the city streets at nights, and at the fact that soap was cheap enough to be used by everyone! So the immigrants continued to pour in. By 1910 it was estimated that 14.5 percent of the people then living in the United States had been born in other countries.

This flood of immigrants worried many Americans. They accused immigrants of taking jobs away from American-born workers, of lowering standards of health and education, and of threatening the country's traditions and way of life by bringing in "un-American" political ideas like anarchism and communism.

The Cliff Dwellers – *a painting that shows the slum conditions in which many immigrants lived.*

Melting pot or salad bowl?

In 1908 Israel Zangwill wrote a play, *The Melting Pot*. The hero, a refugee from persecution in Czarist Russia, escapes to the United States. In the final scene he speaks with enthusiasm about the mixture of peoples in his new homeland:

"America is God's Crucible, the great Melting Pot where all the races of Europe are melting and reforming! . . . Here you stand in your fifty groups with your fifty languages and histories, and your fifty blood hatreds and rivalries, but you won't be like that for long, brothers, for these are the fires of God you've come to – these are the fires of God. . . . German and Frenchman, Irishman and Englishman, Jews and Russians – into the Crucible with you all! God is making the American . . . He will be the fusion of all races, the coming superman."

Zangwill's play was a great success. This was perhaps because many in the audiences who came to see it found its message reassuring. At a time when poor and uneducated immigrants from Europe were flooding into the United States in millions, it was comforting for Americans to be told that their country could turn the newcomers into Americans like themselves.

In fact this never really happeneed, at least not completely. The United States turned out to be more of a salad bowl than a melting pot. Groups from similar national and ethnic backgrounds often stayed together, keeping alive their old identities and many of their old customs. They lived in "Chinatowns" or "Little Italys," areas populated almost entirely by Americans of similar ethnic origins. Such districts can still be found in many large American cities.

Americans from different immigrant backgrounds do mix together in time. It has been estimated, for example, that about 80 percent of the great-grand-children of early-twentieth-century European im-migrants marry outside their own ethnic groups. Yet such third generation Americans often cling with pride to important elements of their ethnic heritage. So do many Americans whose immi-grant origins are even further in the past.

Such accusations were not new. In the 1860s, Chinese workers had been brought to California to build the railroads. The fact that Chinese laborers were willing to work for less pay caused American workers to dislike them. They felt threatened by these people with a different language and a different racial appearance. Chinese communities in the West were attacked and their buildings were burned down. Henry Sienkiewicz, a visitor from Poland, described a scene he witnessed in 1876:

"I was in San Francisco the night a massacre of the Chinese was expected. By the light streaming from burning buildings along the coast marched huge, menacing crowds of workers, carrying banners bearing such inscriptions as the following: 'Self preservation is the first law of nature.' . . . Order was at last restored, but only after the railroads, which had provoked the disturbances by reducing the wages of white men, agreed not to reduce wages and to dismiss their Chinese employees."

In 1882 the strength of anti-Chinese feeling caused Congress to ban most Chinese immigration. Japanese and other Asian immigrants were refused entry as well and by 1924 no Asian immigrants were permitted into the United States. The ban lasted until after the Second World War.

In the 1920s Congress passed laws to limit all kinds of immigration. The one which had most effect was the Reed–Johnson Immigration Act of 1924. This law was an answer to the fears and the prejudices of Americans who were descendants of earlier north European immigrants. It said that in the future no more than 150,000 immigrants a year would be let into the United States. Each country which sent immigrants was given a "quota" which was based on the number of its people already living in the United States. The more it had there already, the more new immigrants it would be allowed to send.

The 1924 system was designed mainly to reduce immigration from southern and eastern Europe. Once it began, 87 percent of the immigration permits went to immigrants from Britain, Ireland, Germany and Scandinavia – the countries from which the ancestors of most 1920s Americans had come.

The 1924 Immigration Act marked the end of one of the most important population movements in the history of the world.

REFORMERS AND PROGRESSIVES

An immigrant family in New York in the early 1900s.

By 1900 the United States was the richest and most productive industrial country in the world. It produced 31.9 percent of the world's coal, 34.1 percent of its iron and 36.7 percent of its steel. About twenty million of its seventy-four million people earned a living from jobs in industry.

Men, women and children labored for long hours in factories, mines and workshops. Many lived in cities, for growing industrial centers like Pittsburgh and Chicago needed more and more workers. The workers' homes were dirty and overcrowded slums. Years later the son of immigrants from an Italian village remembered his mother's unhappiness. He described how she would sit for hours at the window of the family's room in a crowded New York tenement, or apartment building, "staring up at the little patch of sky above the tenements."

Wages were often low. In 1900 the average industrial worker was paid nine dollars for working fifty-nine hours a week. Many worked longer and earned less. In cotton spinning mills the usual working week was sixty-two hours for wages of ten cents an hour. Often the work was unhealthy or dangerous. In one plant belonging to the United States Steel Corporation forty-six men were killed in 1906 – by

burns, explosions, electric shocks, suffocation, falling objects or by being crushed. If workers were killed or injured like this, neither they nor their families received compensation. When the owner of a coal mine was challenged about the dangers and hardships that his workers faced, his reply was short and cruel: "They don't suffer," he said. "Why, they can't even speak English."

Workers tried to form trade, or labor, unions to improve the conditions of their lives. These attempts often failed. One reason for this was the competition for jobs between American-born and immigrant workers. Another was the violent opposition unions faced from employers. Employers would dismiss union members and put their names on a "blacklist." If a worker's name appeared on one of these lists, other employers would refuse to give him a job.

Employers were determined to allow neither their workers nor anyone else to interfere in the way they ran their businesses. Sometimes they persuaded politicians to send soldiers to break up strikes. At other times they hired their own private armies to control their workers. This happened when workers at Andrew Carnegie's Homestead Steel Mill in Pennsylvania went on strike in 1892. The mill's manager hired 300 "detectives" to stop the strike. In

Women and children working in a vegetable cannery.

Samuel Gompers and the A.F.L.

In the early 1900s the leading American labor organization was the American Federation of Labor (A.F.L.). The A.F.L. was formed in 1886 by Samuel Gompers, a leader of the Cigarmakers' Union.

Cigarmaking was a skilled job. Gompers believed that unions of skilled workers were the only ones with a real chance of success. If unskilled workers went on strike they could easily be replaced. Skilled workers could not. This meant that employers would be more likely to listen to them.

The A.F.L. grew steadily as it brought more and more of these skilled workers together – carpenters, printers, iron molders, glassmakers. By 1904 it had 1.75 million members and was the United States' biggest labor organization.

At this time many workers in Europe were joining revolutionary labor movements. These European movements called for the overthrow of capitalism – that is, the private ownership of factories, mines and other means of production – and its replacement by a new socialist economic system.

Most American workers rejected such revolutionary ideas. They were not interested in destroying the existing economic system; they simply wanted to make it work more effectively for their benefit. What they wanted was a bigger share of the wealth they helped to produce. Gompers called this "bread and butter unionism." He believed that unions should concern themselves with the day-to-day welfare of their members, not with politics. Revolutions would not win a better life for working people, he said. But practical demands for higher wages, shorter working hours and safer working conditions would.

clashes between the detectives and the strikers, twenty people were killed.

Employers and the government were not the only enemies labor unions faced. The general public was usually against them. Americans had always seen their country as a land where individuals should be free to improve their lives by their own efforts. Many owned farms, shops or small manufacturing firms. Millions more dreamed of the day when they too would own a farm or a business of their own. Perhaps they might even become rich, as Carnegie had done! People such as these were unlikely to favor organizations which aimed to limit businessmen's freedom of action and opportunities.

But Americans were not complacent about conditions in their country. In the early years of the twentieth century a stream of books and magazine articles drew people's attention to a large number of national problems. Some dealt with conditions of life in the slums of the great cities, some with bribery and corruption in government, others with the dishonesty of wealthy businessmen. The books and articles often brought out startling and shocking facts. This caused some people to describe their authors with contempt as "muckrakers."

One of the best-known muckrakers was Upton Sinclair. In 1906 he attacked the meat-packing industry in his novel *The Jungle*. This gave a horrifying description of life among immigrant workers in the slaughter houses of Chicago. *The Jungle* revealed to many middle-class Americans a side of their nation's life that they hardly knew existed. They were shocked to learn what went into their breakfast sausages. They were even more shocked when government investigators said that what Sinclair had written was correct. Here is part of the investigators' report on conditions in a Chicago meat-packing factory:

"We saw meat shoveled from filthy wooden floors, piled on tables rarely washed, pushed from room to room in rotten boxcarts, in all of which processes it was . . . gathering dirt, splinters, floor filth and the expectoration [spit] of tuberculous and other diseased workers."

Reports like this shocked and frightened the American people. Meat sales dropped by half. The meat companies begged the government to inspect their premises in order to convince people that their products were fit to eat. Congress quickly passed a new federal meat inspection law.

The Strike *by Robert Koehler.*

People began to demand that the nation's leaders should deal with other scandals exposed by the muckrakers. This pressure brought about an important change in American economic and political life. Before 1900 most Americans had believed in "laissez faire" – the idea that governments should interfere with business, and with people's lives in general, as little as possible. After 1900 many Americans became "Progressives." A Progressive was someone who believed that, where necessary, the government should take action to deal with the problems of society.

The Progressive movement found a leader in the Republican Theodore Roosevelt. Roosevelt became President in 1901. One of his main beliefs was that it was the duty of the President to use the power of the federal government to improve conditions of life for the people – to see that the ordinary man and woman got what he called "a square deal."

Roosevelt was particularly concerned about the power of the trusts. His idea was to give the United States the best of both worlds. He wanted to allow businessmen enough freedom of action to make their firms efficient and prosperous, but at the same time to prevent them from taking unfair advantage of

other people. A humorist of the time made fun of this two-sided attitude by describing it in these words:

"The trusts are hideous monsters built up by the enlightened enterprise of the men that have done so much to advance progress in our beloved country. On the one hand I would stamp them under foot, on the other hand, not so fast."

A good example of the "square deal" in action came in 1902. Anthracite coal miners went on strike to obtain better wages and working conditions. Their employers refused even to discuss the workers' demands. Then the President stepped in. He told the mine owners that they were being unreasonable. He said that unless they agreed to negotiate with their workers, the federal government would take control of the coal mines. The threat was enough. The owners changed their attitude and the strike was settled.

Another example of the "square deal" came a few years later. Roosevelt forced the big railroad companies to charge all their customers fair rates, instead of allowing large customers like the oil and meat-packing trusts to pay less than farmers and small businessmen. He also supported laws which compelled manufacturers of foods and medicines to make sure that their products were pure and harmless before selling them.

Theodore Roosevelt retired as President in 1909. In 1912 he tried to regain the position, but he was defeated in the presidential election by Woodrow Wilson, the candidate of the Democratic Party.

Although Roosevelt and Wilson belonged to different political parties, some of their ideas were very similar. Wilson, too, supported the Progressive movement. He had promised that when he became President he would fight "not for the man who has made good [achieved success] but for the man who is going to make good – the man who is knocking and fighting at the closed door of opportunity." As Governor of the state of New Jersey he had fought successfully to make sure that the state was run for the benefit of its people. He had reduced bribery and corruption there, and he had introduced reforms such as laws to give workers compensation for injuries at work.

In March 1913, Wilson stood before the Capitol building in Washington, the home of the United States Congress. There he took the oath as President. Then he made a brief speech about the state of the country: "We have built up a great system of government," he told the crowd which had gathered to watch the ceremony. "But evil has come with the good ... We have squandered [wasted] a great part of what we might have used. We have been proud of our industrial achievements, but we have not hitherto stopped thoughtfully enough to count the human cost ... "

One of these "human costs," Wilson believed, had been the near destruction for many ordinary Americans of a fair chance to get on in life. Workers, farmers, owners of small businesses – people such as these had seen their opportunities steadily shrinking in recent years owing to the continuing growth of the power of "big business" over the nation's economic life. Despite Theodore Roosevelt's attempts to bring the trusts under control, they were even more powerful in 1913 than they had been in 1900. Real equality of opportunity seemed in danger of disappearing in the United States. Wilson believed that only action by the federal government could halt this process. As President, he was determined to see that such action was taken.

Wilson called his policies "The New Freedom." They were put into effect by a series of laws passed between 1913 and 1917. One of Wilson's first steps was to reduce customs duties in order to encourage trade between the United States and other countries. Then he reformed the banking system and introduced a system of federal taxes on high incomes. Other laws reduced the powers of the trusts, gave more rights to labor unions and made it easier for farmers to borrow money from the federal government to develop their land. Many individual states also passed Progressive laws. They forbade factories to employ children, introduced secret voting, improved safety at work, and protected their natural resources.

But not all Wilson's plans of reform were accepted. For example, the Senate refused to pass a law giving the federal authorities more control over the buying and selling of business shares. Another law, stopping child labor in factories everywhere, was declared to be unconstitutional by the Supreme Court.

The Progressive movement changed and improved American life in many ways. But many people still distrusted too much government "interference" in the nation's life.

Theodore Roosevelt and conservation

Perhaps Theodore Roosevelt's most important service to his country was to persuade Congress to pass a number of conservation laws. These were laws to save the country's natural resources from being used up carelessly and greedily.

The United States desperately needed such laws in the early 1900s. Roosevelt pointed out that unless action were taken to slow down the destruction of the country's forests, mineral resources and soil fertility, Americans would soon discover that much of the natural wealth of the United States had been destroyed for ever.

Congress listened to Roosevelt's advice. It passed conservation laws under which millions of acres of land were protected and their forest and mineral wealth preserved for the use of future generations.

20

AN AMERICAN EMPIRE

The Maine *exploding in Havana harbor in February, 1898.*

On January 25, 1898, one of the most modern ships in the United States' navy steamed into the harbor of Havana, Cuba. The ship was a cruiser called the *Maine*. A war was being fought in Cuba at this time and the *Maine* had been sent to Havana as a demonstration of American power. Three weeks later, on the night of February 15, a huge explosion shook the city. The *Maine* was blown to pieces and 260 of its crew were killed.

To this day, the cause of the explosion that destroyed the *Maine* remains a mystery. Some believe that it was set off by an accidental spark in the ship's magazine, or ammunition store. At the time, however, many Americans believed that the explosion had been caused by an enemy mine.

The man who made this claim most loudly was a newspaper owner named William Randolph Hearst. "THE WARSHIP *MAINE* WAS SPLIT IN TWO BY AN ENEMY'S INFERNAL [hellish] MACHINE," read the headline in one of his newspapers on February 17. The story which followed made it clear that to Hearst the "enemy" in the headline was Spain. Most Americans agreed with him. This was not because they had any proof. It was because they wanted to believe it. Let us see why.

In 1867 the United States had bought Alaska from Russia. Apart from this it had brought no additional land under its rule since gaining control of California and the Southwest in the Mexican War of 1846 to 1848. In the 1890s, however, a new spirit started to enter American foreign policy. These were years when Britain, France and Germany were busy claiming colonies, foreign lands which they could rule and exploit. Some Americans believed that the United States should do the same. Colonies overseas meant trade, wealth, power and prestige. "A policy of isolation did well enough [was all right] when we were an embryo nation, but today things are different," said Senator Orville Platt in 1893. "We are the most advanced and powerful nation on earth and our future demands an abandonment of the policy of isolation. It is to the ocean our children must look, as they once looked to the boundless west."

Many Americans agreed with Platt. Politicians, businessmen, newspapers and missionaries joined together to claim that "the Anglo-Saxon race" – by which they meant Americans as well as North Europeans – had a right and a duty to bring western civilization to the peoples of Asia, Africa and Latin

Monroe's Doctrine

In the early nineteenth century most of Central and South America, or Latin America, was ruled by Spain. In the 1820s these Spanish colonies rebelled.

The Spanish government asked the great powers of Europe to help it to defeat the rebels. When Americans heard this they were alarmed. They did not want the armies and navies of powerful European nations in their part of the world. The rebel Spanish colonies were the United States' nearest neighbors. Americans felt that it was important to their country's safety to make sure that no foreign enemies gained influence in them.

In 1823 President Monroe warned European nations not to interfere in Latin American affairs. "The American continents are henceforth not to be considered as subjects for future colonization by European powers," Monroe told Congress. "We should consider any attempt on their part to extend their system to any portion of this hemisphere [half of the world] as dangerous to our peace and safety."

Monroe's statement came to be called the "Monroe Doctrine." It became one of the most important ideas in American foreign policy.

America. How? By making them accept "Anglo-Saxon" rule or guidance.

From 1895 onwards feelings of this kind were focused more and more upon Cuba, which lay only ninety miles from the American coast. Many Americans had invested money in sugar and tobacco plantations there. But at this time Cuba was a Spanish colony.

In 1895 the people of Cuba rose in rebellion against their Spanish rulers. The rebels raided and burned villages, sugar plantations and railroad depots. To cut off the rebels' supplies, Spanish soldiers moved thousands of Cuban civilians into prison camps. The camps became badly overcrowded. As many as 200,000 people died in them of disease and hunger.

Hearst and another American newspaper owner named Joseph Pulitzer published sensational accounts of the struggle in Cuba. Day after day millions of Americans read how, according to Hearst and Pulitzer, Cubans were being badly treated by the Spaniards. By 1898 many Americans felt that the United States should do something to help the Cubans. It was to show its sympathy for the rebels that the American government sent the *Maine* to Havana.

When the *Maine* blew up, people began calling for war with Spain. "Remember the *Maine*" became a battle cry. In April President McKinley demanded that Spain should withdraw from Cuba, and a few days later Spain and the United States went to war.

The Spanish–American War was fought in two parts of the world. One was Cuba; the other was the Philippines.

The Philippines was another big Spanish colony near the coast of Southeast Asia. It was said that President McKinley had to search a globe to find out exactly where it was. But he saw that the islands would be useful for the United States to control. From bases in the Philippines American soldiers and sailors would be able to protect the growing number of American traders in China.

– And Roosevelt's Corollary

The original Monroe Doctrine told Europeans not to interfere in Latin America. In 1904 President Theodore Roosevelt made an addition, or "corollary" to it. He said that the United States would intervene there whenever it thought necessary. Roosevelt believed that by doing this the United States would be able to ensure the internal stability of its Latin American neighbors and so remove any excuse for Europeans to interfere in their affairs.

In the next twenty years American governments often acted upon Roosevelt's Corollary. American soldiers landed in countries like Nicaragua, Haiti and the Dominican Republic, and took over their governments for years at a time. Often the Americans made big improvements – paying off debts, draining swamps, building roads. But this did not stop Latin Americans from resenting their interference.

Spanish General Toral surrendering to U.S. General Shafter, July 13, 1898.

The first battle of the Spanish–American War was fought in the Philippines. American warships sank a Spanish fleet that was anchored there. A few weeks later American soldiers occupied Manila, the chief city in the Philippines, and Spanish resistance came to an end.

American soldiers also landed in Cuba. In less than two weeks of fighting, the Spanish were again defeated. Other American soldiers occupied Puerto Rico, another Spanish-owned island close to Cuba. In July the Spanish government saw it was beaten. It asked the Americans for peace.

When peace was signed, Spain gave most of its overseas empire to the United States – Cuba, the Philippines, Puerto Rico and a small Pacific island called Guam. At the same time the United States also annexed Hawaii. Hawaii was a group of islands in the middle of the Pacific Ocean. Before this it had been independent, but Americans owned profitable sugar and pineapple plantations there.

In less than a year the United States had become a colonial power, with millions of non-Americans under its rule. Some Americans were worried by this. After all, they, too, had once been a colonial people. In rebelling against British rule they had claimed that colonial peoples should be free to rule themselves. So what about the Cubans? And what about the Filipinos? Filipinos who had fought for independence from Spain were soon fighting against American occupation troops. How could Americans fight against such people without being unfaithful to the most important traditions and values of their own country?

Most Americans answered this question by claiming that they were preparing underdeveloped nations for civilization and democracy. "I'm proud of my country," said a Methodist minister in New England, "patiently teaching people to govern themselves and to enjoy the blessings of a Christian civilization. Surely this Spanish war has not been a grab for empire, but an heroic effort to free the oppressed and to teach millions of ignorant, debased human beings how to live."

There was some truth in the clergyman's claim. The Americans built schools and hospitals, constructed roads, provided pure water supplies and put an end to killer diseases like malaria and yellow fever in the lands they now ruled. They continued to rule most of them until the middle years of the century. The Philippines became an independent country in 1946. In 1953 Puerto Rico became self-governing, but continued to be closely tied to the United States. In 1959 Hawaii was admitted as the fiftieth state of the Union.

Cuba was treated differently. When Congress declared war on Spain in 1898 it said that it was only doing so to help the Cuban people to win independence. When the war ended, Cuba was soon declared an independent country.

But for years Cuba's independence was just a pretense. Before the Americans took away their soldiers in 1902 they made the Cuban government give them land at Guantanamo Bay on the Cuban coast. A big American naval base was built there. The Cubans also had to accept a condition called the Platt Amendment. This said that the United States could send troops to take control of Cuba any time it believed that American interests were in danger – in other words, whenever it wanted.

It did so many times. In 1906, for example, President Theodore Roosevelt set up an American military government in Cuba to stop a revolution. This ran the country's affairs until 1909. In 1912, 1917 and 1921 American marines were again sent to stop revolutions in Cuba. For many years the country continued to be little more than a protectorate of the United States.

Dollar Diplomacy

In economic and business affairs the United States has long been strongly internationalist. American foreign policy has often tried to provide business-men with fresh opportunities. In the early years of the twentieth century, for example, the in-dustrial nations of Europe were dividing the trade of China between them. To ensure that Americans also profited from this rich new market the United States' government worked to ensure freedom of trade in China by persuading other nations to accept a policy called the "Open Door."

The close relationship between American foreign policy and American business interests has shown itself in other ways. Political leaders have some-times encouraged American businesses to invest abroad as a way of strengthening the political position of the United States. This happened in the early 1900s, when President Taft favored a policy known as "Dollar Diplomacy." This en-couraged Americans to invest in areas that were strategically important to the United States, such as Latin America.

American firms which have established themselves in other countries have often received a mixed welcome. Their critics accuse them of using their economic power to influence foreign governments to follow policies that serve the political and economic interests of the United States rather than those of the country in which they are working. But foreign leaders often welcome American investment. They see such investment as a way of obtaining new jobs and new technology, and so of improving their countries' living standards.

"I took Panama"

In the early 1900s the American government wanted to build a canal across the Isthmus of Panama. The isthmus is the neck of land that joins North and South America and separates the Caribbean Sea from the Pacific Ocean. Building a canal across it would mean that American ships could travel quickly between the east and west coasts of the United States instead of having to make a long sea journey around South America.

The main problem was that the United States did not own the isthmus; a Latin American country called Colombia did. In 1903, when the Colombian government was slow to give the Americans permission to build the canal, President Theodore Roosevelt sent warships to Panama. The warships helped a small group of Panamanian businessmen to rebel against the Colombian government.

The rebels declared that Panama was now an independent state. A few days later they gave the Americans control over a ten-and-a-half-mile-wide strip of land called the Canal Zone across their new country. The way was clear for the Americans to build their canal. They began dig-ging in 1904 and the first ships steamed through the completed canal in 1914.

Most Latin Americans thought that the Panama rebellion had been organized by Roosevelt. They thought so even more when he openly boasted: "I took Panama."

The building of the Panama Canal.

TWENTIETH CENTURY AMERICANS

—— 21 ——
A WAR AND A PEACE

A British propaganda poster.

In August 1914, a war started on the continent of Europe. It was the beginning of a struggle that lasted for more than four years, brought death to millions of people and changed the history of the world. At the time people called the conflict the Great War. Later it was called the First World War.

The main countries fighting the war were, on one side, France, Great Britain and Russia. They were known as the Allies. On the other side the main countries were Germany and Austria, who were called the Central Powers.

Most Americans wanted to keep out of the war. They saw it as a purely European affair that was not their concern. When President Wilson said that they should be "impartial in thought as well as in action," most people were ready to agree with him.

But Americans found it difficult to stay impartial for long. In the first days of the war the German government sent its armies marching into neutral Belgium. This shocked many Americans. They were even more shocked when newspapers printed reports – often false or exaggerated – of German cruelty towards Belgian civilians.

From the very beginning of the war the strong British navy prevented German ships from trading with the United States. But trade between the United States and the Allies grew quickly. By 1915 American factories were making vast quantities of weapons and munitions and selling them to Britain and France.

German leaders were determined to stop this flow of armaments to their enemies. They announced in February 1915, that they would sink all Allied merchant ships in the seas around the British Isles. On a hazy afternoon in May, a big British passenger ship called the *Lusitania* was nearing the end of its voyage from the United States to Britain. Suddenly, without any warning, it was hit by a torpedo from a German submarine. Within minutes the *Lusitania* was sinking. More than 1,000 passengers went with it to the bottom of the ocean. One hundred and twenty-eight of those passengers were Americans.

The sinking of the *Lusitania* made Americans very angry. Some began to think that Germany would do anything to win the war. But most still wanted peace. President Wilson made strong protests to the German government. For a time the Germans stopped the submarine attacks.

In the autumn of 1916 American voters re-elected Wilson as President, mainly because he had kept them out of the war. In January 1917, Wilson made a speech to Congress. In it he appealed to the warring nations of Europe to settle their differences and make "a peace without victory." This, he said, was the only kind of peace that could last.

But by now American bankers had lent a lot of money to the Allies. And American military supplies were still pouring across the Atlantic. Germany's war leaders feared that, unless the flow of supplies was stopped, their country would be defeated. Only nine days after Wilson's speech they again ordered their submarines to begin sinking ships sailing towards Allied ports. This time the order included neutral vessels.

A poster recruiting soldiers to fight for "Uncle Sam."

In the next few weeks German submarines sank five American ships. With German torpedoes sending American sailors to their deaths in the grey waters of the Atlantic, Wilson felt that he had no choice. On April 2, 1917, he asked Congress to declare war on

The Zimmermann telegram

At the beginning of 1917 many Americans were still strongly against becoming involved in the First World War. To people on the Great Plains, in Texas or in California, Europe seemed very far away. European quarrels, they believed, were none of their business.

Then, on March 1, 1917, newspapers all over the United States printed a sensational story. The story claimed that Arthur Zimmermann, the German Foreign Secretary, had tried to persuade Mexico and Japan to attack the United States.

The affair had begun on January 16. Zimmermann had sent a secret telegram to the German ambassador in Mexico. The telegram told the ambassador to invite the Mexican government to sign an alliance with Germany. The idea was that if the United States went to war with Germany, the Mexicans should attack the Americans from the south. Mexico's reward would be the return of all the lands it had lost to the United States in 1848. Zimmermann also wanted Mexico to invite Japan to join the anti-American alliance.

Zimmermann's telegram was intercepted and decoded by British agents. On February 24, when Americans were already angry at Germany for starting submarine attacks again, the British gave Wilson a copy of the telegram. Wilson was furious. He told the newspapers. People who wanted to keep the United States out of the war, and those who favored Germany, said that the telegram was a forgery, a British trick. But their efforts to claim that the story was untrue collapsed when Zimmermann himself said: "It is true."

The Zimmermann telegram turned American opinion more strongly in favor of the Allies. This was especially true in the previously uninterested western parts of the country. These were the very areas that would have been threatened most if Zimmermann's plan had worked.

Victory Won by Childe Hassan, painted to celebrate the end of the First World War.

Germany. Wilson's aim was not simply to defeat Germany. He saw the war as a great crusade to ensure the future peace of the world. For him the war would become a war "to make the world safe for democracy, the war to end all wars."

When the United States declared war on Germany the American army was a small force of only 200,000 soldiers. Millions more men had to be recruited, trained, equipped and shipped across the Atlantic to Europe. All this took time. A full year passed before many American soldiers were available to help the European Allies.

In the spring of 1918 the German armies began a last desperate offensive against the French and the British. Their aim was to win the war before the new American army was ready to fight. By July they were within a few miles of Paris.

The Allies were in great danger. They placed all their armies under one commander, the French general Foch. Luckily for Foch, American soldiers began to arrive at the battlefront to strengthen his forces. Soon over a million of them had joined in the battles against the Germans.

In August 1918, the Allied armies counter-attacked. The German armies were driven back towards their own frontiers. In October the German government asked for peace. On November 11, 1918, German and Allied leaders signed an armistice, an agreement to stop fighting. The bloodiest and most destructive war the world had ever known was over.

By January 1919, President Wilson was in Europe. He was there to help to work out a peace treaty. He was greeted by cheering crowds in the Allied capitals and spoken of as "Wilson the Just."

But when Wilson met other Allied leaders to work out the details of the treaty, the welcome became less friendly. The French leader, Georges Clemenceau, thought that Wilson lacked experience in international affairs. Worse still, the American President did not seem to realize this. "How can I talk to a fellow who thinks himself the first man in two thousand years to know anything about peace on earth?" asked Clemenceau.

Both Wilson and Clemenceau wanted to make sure that a war like the First World War never happened again. Wilson wanted to do this by writing a treaty that did not leave the Germans with lots of grievances. He believed that if the Germans thought they had not been treated fairly, they might one day start a war of revenge. Clemenceau thought differently. He believed there was only one way to make a peace that would last. The Germans had to be made so weak that they would never have the strength to fight again.

After much arguing, and without consulting the Germans, the Allied leaders agreed on a peace treaty. They called it the Versailles Treaty, after the palace near Paris where it was signed in May 1919.

The Versailles Treaty was harder in its treatment of the Germans than Wilson had wanted. Among other things it made them take all the blame for the war. It also made them agree to pay for all the damage that the war had caused. These "reparation" payments were fixed at many millions of dollars.

Wilson was disappointed with much of the Versailles Treaty. But he returned to the United States with high hopes for part of it. This was a scheme that he believed could still make his dream of a world without war come true. It was a plan to set up a League of Nations.

The signing of the peace treaty at Versailles.

The League of Nations was to be an organization where representatives of the world's nations would meet and settle their differences by discussion instead of war. It had taken Wilson months of hard bargaining to persuade the other Allied leaders to accept this plan. Now he faced a battle to persuade Congress and the American people to accept it, too.

Wilson knew that this would not be easy. Many Americans were against their country becoming permanently involved in the problems of Europe. And they were suspicious of the League of Nations. Wouldn't joining such an organization mean that the United States might be dragged into quarrels, perhaps even wars, that were none of its business?

Wilson tried to remove such fears. But as the months passed it began to seem that he was failing to do so. After another trip to Europe he returned to America, tired and ill. But he boarded a special train and set off on a speaking tour of the western United States to plead for the League.

The tour was never completed. On September 25, 1919, the exhausted Wilson suffered a severe stroke.

He was taken back to Washington, his health broken for ever. In March 1920, the Senate voted against the United States joining the League of Nations, and the idea was dropped.

From his invalid's armchair in the White House a sick and disappointed Wilson spoke the last words on the subject. "We had a chance to gain the leadership of the world. We have lost it and soon we shall be witnessing the tragedy of it all."

Wilson's Fourteen Points

President Wilson always insisted that the United States was fighting the First World War not against the German people but against their warlike leaders. In January 1918, he outlined his ideas for a just and lasting peace in a speech to the United States Senate. These ideas were called the Fourteen Points.

Among other things, Wilson's Fourteen Points required nations to stop making secret agreements, to reduce their military forces and armaments, to trade freely with one another and to draw up new national boundaries that would allow the separate peoples of Europe to rule themselves. It was in the Fourteen Points, also, that Wilson first suggested the League of Nations.

When the German government asked for peace in October 1918, it hoped that the Allies would base their terms on the Fourteen Points. But other Allied leaders regarded some of Wilson's ideas as idealistic nonsense. The French leader, Clemenceau, compared the Fourteen Points sarcastically to the Christian religion's Ten Commandments. "Mr. Wilson bores me with his Fourteen Points," he grumbled. "Why, God Almighty has only ten!"

In the end the Fourteen Points had much less influence on the terms of the Versailles Treaty than Wilson had hoped for. Some people still believe that this was a tragedy. They say that the post-war world would have been a better and a safer place if the Fourteen Points had been followed more closely. Others disagree. They believe that the world would have been safer if the Fourteen Points had been less closely followed!

THE ROARING TWENTIES

Dancing the Charleston in the "roaring twenties."

Girls dancing the Charleston. Gangsters carrying machine guns. Charlie Chaplin playing comical tricks. These are some of the pictures that come into people's minds when they think of the United States in the 1920s. The "roaring twenties." Good times. Wild times.

The United States was very rich in these years. Because of the First World War, other countries owed it a lot of money. It had plenty of raw materials and plenty of factories. Its national income – the total earnings of all its citizens – was much higher, than that of Britain, France, Germany and Japan put together.

American factories produced more goods every year. The busiest were those making automobiles. Between 1922 and 1927, the number of cars on the roads rose from under eleven million to over twenty million. The electrical industry also prospered. It made hundreds of thousands of refrigerators, vacuum cleaners, stoves and radios.

The United States became the first nation in history to build its way of life on selling vast quantities of goods that gave ordinary people easier and more enjoyable lives. These "consumer goods" poured off the assembly lines of big new factories. Between 1919 and 1929 such mass-production factories doubled their output.

The growth of industry made many Americans well-off. Millions earned good wages. Thousands invested money in successful firms so that they could share in their profits. Many bought cars, radios and other new products with their money. Often they obtained these goods by paying a small deposit and agreeing to pay the rest of the cost through an "instalment plan." Their motto was "Live now, pay tomorrow" – a tomorrow which most were convinced would be like today only better, with even more money swelling their wallets.

Businessmen became popular heroes in the 1920s. Men like Henry Ford were widely admired as the creators of the nation's prosperity. "The man who builds a factory builds a temple," said Calvin Coolidge, the President from 1923 to 1929. "The man who works there, worships there."

Coolidge's words help to explain the policies of American governments in the 1920s. These governments were controlled by the Republican Party. Republicans believed that if the government looked after the interests of the businessman, everybody would become richer. Businessmen whose firms were doing well, they claimed, would take on more workers and pay more wages. In this way their growing wealth would benefit everybody.

To help businessmen Congress placed high import taxes on goods from abroad. The aim was to make imported goods more expensive, so that American manufacturers would have less competition from foreign rivals. At the same time Congress reduced taxes on high incomes and company profits. This gave rich men more money to invest.

Sacco and Vanzetti

In 1917 a communist revolution had taken place in Russia. Some Americans feared that revolutionaries, or "reds," were plotting a similar take-over in the United States. A"red scare" began. People who criticized the way American society was organized risked being accused of disloyalty. This risk was especially great for anyone who supported socialist ideas. Such ideas were thought to be foreign and "un-American." People who held them were feared and persecuted, especially if they were foreign-born.

On April 15, 1920, two people were shot dead in a $15,000 robbery near Boston. Witnesses said that two of the robbers looked "very Italian." Three weeks later two Italian immigrants named Nicola Sacco and Bartolomeo Vanzetti were arrested.

Both had alibis for the time of the murder. But Sacco owned a gun that could have been used in the killings. Both men were dark-skinned and looked Italian. And both were foreigners who held left-wing political ideas. The judge at their trial disliked all these things. He told friends that he was going to get "those anarchist bastards," and eventually sentenced both Sacco and Vanzetti to death.

Many believed that Sacco and Vanzetti had been condemned for their origins and political beliefs, not because of the evidence against them. For six years people both in the United States and abroad fought for their release. On August 22, 1927, however, both men were executed.

Sacco and Vanzetti protested to the end that they were innocent. To this day neither the guilt nor the innocence of Sacco and Vanzetti has been finally proved. But their case is remembered as an example of how racial and political prejudice may cause justice to suffer.

Yet there were lots of poor Americans. A survey in 1929 showed that half the American people had hardly enough money to buy sufficient food and clothing. In the industrial cities of the North, such as Chicago and Pittsburgh, immigrant workers still labored long hours for low wages in steel mills, factories and slaughter houses. In the South thousands of poor farmers, both black and white, worked from sunrise to sunset to earn barely enough to live on. The wealth that Republicans said would benefit everybody never reached people like these.

The main reason for poverty among industrial workers was low wages. Farmers and farm workers had a hard time for different reasons. In the South many farmers did not own the land they farmed. They were sharecroppers. For rent, a sharecropper gave the landowner part of what he grew – often so much that he was left with hardly enough to feed his family.

In the West most farmers owned their land. But they, too, faced hard times. During the First World War they had been able to sell their wheat to Europe for high prices. By 1921, however, the countries of Europe no longer needed so much American food.

And farmers were finding it more difficult to sell their produce at home. Immigration had fallen, so the number of people needing food was growing more slowly. All the new cars didn't help either. Cars ran on gasoline, not on corn and hay like horses.

American farmers found themselves growing products they could not sell. By 1924, around 600,000 of them were bankrupt.

But to Americans who owned shares or "stock," in industrial companies the future looked bright. Sales of consumer goods went on rising. This meant bigger profits for the firms that made them. This in turn sent up the value of shares in such firms.

In 1928 the American people elected a new President, Herbert Hoover. Hoover was sure that American prosperity would go on growing and that the poverty in which some Americans still lived would be remembered as something in the past. He said that there would soon be "a chicken in every pot and two cars in every garage."

Looking at the way their standard of living had risen during the 1920s, many other Americans thought the same.

City Activities *by Thomas Hart Benton. The artist gives his view of American society in the 1920s.*

The movies

In the 1920s American movies filled the cinema screens of the world. Most were made in Hollywood, a suburb of the city of Los Angeles in California. Hollywood's big attraction for film-makers was its clean air and plentiful sunshine. The movies made there were bright and clear. By the 1920s it had become the film-making capital of the world.

Hollywood movies were made by large companies called studios. The men who ran these studios were businessmen and their main aim was to make as much money as possible. They soon found that one way to do this was to standardize their films. When audiences had shown that they liked a certain kind of film, the studios made many more of exactly the same kind.

Another sure way for a studio to make money was to turn its actors into "stars." Stars were actors who were so popular that people went in crowds to see any film they appeared in, no matter how good or bad it was. A famous star could make any movie a certain success. So the studios went to great lengths to make their actors into stars. They encouraged fan magazines. They set up special publicity departments to get stories about their actors into the newspapers.

The movies of the 1920s were silent. They spoke in pictures, not words, and so their language was international. All over the world, from Berlin to Tokyo, from London to Buenos Aires, tens of millions of people lined up every night of the week to see their favorite Hollywood stars—and, without realizing it, to be Americanized.

Hollywood movies showed people a world that was more exciting, more free, more equal, than their own. To most people this world of the movies remained a dream world, separate from real life. But to some it became more. It made them realize, however dimly, that perhaps their own conditions of life could be improved.

Al Capone and the bootleggers

In 1919 the American people voted in favor of a new amendment to the Constitution. The Eighteenth Amendment prohibited the making or selling of alcoholic drinks in the United States. People who supported "prohibition" claimed that it would stop alcoholism and drunkenness and make the United States a healthier, happier country.

But many Americans were not willing to give up alcoholic drinks. Millions began to break the prohibition law deliberately and regularly. Illegal drinking places called "speakeasies" opened in basements and backrooms all over the country. The city of Chicago had 10,000 of them. New York had 32,000.

Speakeasies obtained their alcoholic drinks from criminals called "bootleggers." Bootleggers worked together in gangs or "mobs." The best-known mob was one in Chicago led by the gangster "Scarface" Al Capone.

Bootlegging was a dangerous business. Competition between rival mobs sometimes caused bloody street wars, fought out with armored cars and machine guns. The winners of the gangster wars became rich and powerful. They used their wealth to bribe police and other public officials to do nothing about their law-breaking. Al Capone became the real ruler of Chicao. He had a private army of nearly a thousand thugs equipped with machine guns. His income was over 100 million dollars a year.

By the end of the 1920s most Americans regarded prohibition as half scandal, half joke. The dis-

Prohibition. A carefully posed photograph showing federal agents examining some of the bottles of liquor they have discovered hidden in a coal steamer in New York harbor.

honesty and corruption which grew with it made them lose their respect both for the law and for the people who were supposed to enforce it. Prohibition was finally given up in 1933. But it had done the United States lasting harm. It made law-breaking a habit for many otherwise respectable Americans. And gangsters remained powerful. Many used the money they had made as bootleggers to set up other criminal businesses.

23

CRASH AND DEPRESSION

In the heart of New York City lies a narrow street enclosed by the walls of high office buildings. Its name is Wall Street.

One Thursday afternoon in October 1929, a workman outside an upper floor window of a Wall Street office found himself staring into the eyes of four policemen. They reached out to catch hold of him. "Don't jump!" shouted one of the policemen. "It's not that bad." "Who's going to jump?" asked the surprised worker. "I'm just washing windows!"

To understand this incident we need to look at what had been happening in Wall Street in the months and years before that October afternoon in 1929.

Wall Street is the home of the New York Stock Exchange. Here dealers called stockbrokers buy and sell valuable pieces of paper. The pieces of paper are share certificates. Each certificate represents a certain amount of money invested in a company.

Every year in the 1920s the sales of cars, radios and other consumer goods rose. This meant bigger profits for the firms which made them. This in turn sent up the value of shares in such firms.

Owning shares in a business gives you the right to a share of its profits. But you can make money from shares in another way. You can buy them at one price, then, if the company does well, sell them later at a higher one.

More and more people were eager to get some of this easy money. By 1929 buying and selling shares – "playing the market" – had become almost a national hobby. You could see this from the rise in the number of shares changing hands. In 1923 the number was 236 million; by 1928 it had grown to 1,125 million.

Like most other things in the United States in the 1920s, you could buy shares on credit. A hundred dollars cash would "buy" a thousand dollars' worth of shares from any stockbroker. Many people borrowed large amounts of money from the banks to buy shares in this way – "on the margin", as it was called.

Wall Street out of control in early October 1929. This cartoon accurately predicted the stock market crash that occurred three weeks later.

Most of these "on the margin" share buyers were really gamblers. Their idea was to spot shares that would quickly rise in value, buy them at one price and then resell at a higher one a few weeks later. They could then pay back the bank, having made a quick profit.

By the fall of 1929 the urge to buy shares had become a sort of fever. Prices went up and up. One visitor to Wall Street was reminded of a street fight, as stockbrokers pushed and scrambled to buy shares for their customers.

Yet some people began to have doubts. The true value of shares in a business firm depends upon its profits. By the fall of 1929 the profits being made by many American firms had been decreasing for some time. If profits were falling, thought more cautious investors, then share prices, too, would soon fall. Slowly, such people began to sell their shares. Day by day their numbers grew. Soon so many people were selling shares that prices did start to fall.

At first many investors held on to their shares, hoping that prices would rise again. But the fall became faster. A panic began. On Thursday, October 24, 1929 – Black Thursday – 13 million shares were sold. On the following Tuesday, October 29 – Terrifying Tuesday – 16.5 million were sold.

By the end of the year the value of all shares had dropped by $40,000 million. Thousands of people, especially those who had borrowed to buy on the margin, found themselves facing debt and ruin. Some committed suicide. This was what the policemen thought that the window cleaner was planning.

This collapse of American share prices was known as the Wall Street Crash. It marked the end of the prosperity of the 1920s.

"What has gone wrong?" people asked. Some blamed the blindness of politicians for the Crash, others the greed of investors and stockbrokers. But it had a more important cause. The fact was that by the end of the 1920s not enough people were buying the products of America's expanded industries. Why? Because too little of the United States' increased wealth was finding its way into the hands of the country's workers and farmers. The most important cause of the Wall Street Crash was simply this – that too few Americans were earning enough money to buy the goods that they themselves were producing.

The Crash made people uncertain about the future. Many decided to save any money they had instead of spending it on such things as new cars and radios. American factories were already making more goods than they could sell. Now they had even fewer customers.

A breadline. Unemployed people line up for food rations in Times Square, New York, in the early 1930s.

The Crash affected their sales to foreign countries, too. In the 1920s American goods had sold well overseas, especially in Europe. But countries such as Britain and Germany had not prospered after the war as the United States had. They had often paid for their purchases with money borrowed from American banks. After the Wall Street Crash the banks wanted their money back. European buyers became short of cash and American overseas sales dried up almost completely. Goods piled up unsold in factory warehouses. Employers stopped employing workers and reduced production.

By the end of 1931 nearly eight million Americans were out of work. Unlike unemployed workers in countries such as Germany and Britain, they received no government unemployment pay. Many were soon without homes or food and had to live on charity. Millions spent hours shuffling slowly forward in "breadlines." Here they received free pieces of bread or bowls of soup, paid for by money collected from those who could afford it.

By 1932 the position was worse still. Thousands of banks and over 100,000 businesses had closed down. Industrial production had fallen by half and wage payments by 60 percent. New investment in industry was down by 90 percent. Twelve million people, one out of every four of the country's workers, were unemployed. The city of Chicago alone had almost three-quarters of a million workers without jobs. This was four out of ten of its normal working population. The position was just as bad in other places.

The Depression was easiest to see in the towns, with their silent factories, closed shops and slowly moving breadlines. But it brought ruin and despair to the farmlands also. Farmers simply could not sell their produce. With the number of people out of work rising day by day, their customers in the cities could no longer afford to buy. If anyone did buy, it was at the lowest possible prices. The same was true of the farmers' overseas customers.

Many farmers grew desperate. They took out shotguns and banded together to drive away men who came to throw them off their farms for not paying their debts. How can we pay, the farmers asked, when nobody will give us a fair price for our crops? They paraded through the streets in angry

"You walk"

A writer described what it was like to be jobless and homeless in an American city in the early 1930s:

"You get shoved out early; you get your coffee and start walking. A couple of hours before noon you get in line. You eat and start walking. At night you sleep where you can. You don't talk. You eat what you can. You walk. No one talks to you. You walk. It's cold, and you shiver and stand in doorways or sit in railroad stations. You don't see much. You forget. You walk an hour and forget where you started from. It is day, and then it's night, and then it's day again. And you don't remember which was first. You walk."

processions. They waved placards with words such as: "In Hoover we trusted, now we are busted."

By 1932 people of every kind – factory workers, farmers, office workers, store keepers – were demanding that President Hoover take stronger action to deal with the Depression.

Hoover believed that he could do two things to end the Depression. The first was to "balance the budget" – that is, to make sure that the government's spending did not exceed its income. The second was to restore businessmen's confidence in the future, so that they would begin to take on workers again.

Time and time again in the early 1930s Hoover told people that recovery from the Depression was "just around the corner." But the factories remained closed. The breadlines grew longer. People became hungrier. To masses of unemployed workers Hoover seemed uncaring and unable to help them.

Then, Franklin D. Roosevelt came on the scene. Roosevelt was the Governor of the state of New York. Years earlier he had been crippled by polio. But in 1932 the Democratic Party chose him to run against President Hoover in that year's election for a new president.

Roosevelt gave an impression of energy and determination, and of caring deeply for the welfare of ordinary people. All over the United States anxious men and women felt that here at last was a man who understood their troubles, who sympathized with them – and, most important of all, who sounded as if he would do something to help them.

Roosevelt's main idea was that the federal government should take the lead in the fight against the Depression. He told the American people: "The country needs and demands bold, persistent experimentation. Above all try something." He promised them a "New Deal."

Hoover condemned Roosevelt's policies of greater government action. He was sure that such policies would only make things worse. They would, he said, "destroy the very foundations of our American system." They would cause people to lose their ability to stand on their own feet and bear their own responsibilities. If they were introduced, he prophesied grimly, "grass will grow in the streets of a hundred cities, a thousand towns."

The majority of the American people ignored Hoover's gloomy warnings. On November 9, 1932, they elected Franklin Roosevelt as the next President of the United States by the largest majority in American history. In only six of the nation's forty-eight states did Hoover gain a majority of the votes. In the other forty-two states the people chose Roosevelt.

The bonus army

In the spring of 1932 thousands of unemployed ex-servicemen poured into Washington, the nation's capital. They wanted the government to give them some bonus payments that it owed them from the war years. The newspapers called them the "bonus army."

The men of the bonus army were determined to stay in Washington until the President did something to help them. They set up a camp of rough shelters and huts on the edge of the city. Similar camps could be found on rubbish dumps outside every large American city by this time. The homeless people who lived in them named their camps "Hoovervilles," after the President.

Soldiers and police attacking the "bonus army" camp in Washington D.C. in 1932.

This gathering of desperate men alarmed President Hoover. He ordered soldiers and the police to burn their camp and drive them out of Washington. As the smoke billowed up from the burning huts of the bonus army, a government spokesman defended Hoover's decision. He said that in the circumstances "only two courses were left open to the President" – that is, that the President could do only one of two things: "One was to surrender the government to the mob. The other was to uphold law and order and suppress [crush] the mob."

An anonymous poet took a different view of what had happened:

Only two courses were open,
As anyone can see:
To vindicate law and order
Or yield to anarchy.
Granted! – the Chiefs of Government
Cannot tolerate mobs –
But isn't it strange you never thought
Of giving the workless jobs?

Only two courses were open –
When men who had fought for you
Starved in the streets of our cities,
Finding no work to do –
When in the richest of the countries
Babies wept unfed –
Strange it never occurred to you
To give the hungry bread!

99

ROOSEVELT'S NEW DEAL

On a cold, grey Saturday in March 1933, Franklin D. Roosevelt took the oath as President of the United States. For a hundred days, from March 8 to June 16 he sent Congress a flood of proposals for new laws. The American people had asked for action. In the "Hundred Days" Roosevelt gave it to them.

Many of the new laws set up government organizations called "agencies" to help the nation to recover from the Depression. The Civilian Conservation Corps (CCC) found work for many thousands of young men. The Federal Emergency Relief Administration (FERA) gave individual states government money to help their unemployed and

YEARS OF DUST

RESETTLEMENT ADMINISTRATION
Rescues Victims
Restores Land to Proper Use

Years of Dust *by Ben Shahn.*

Roosevelt and the farmers

In April 1933, a few weeks after Roosevelt became President, American newspapers printed a disturbing story. The story came from the western farming state of Iowa. It told of a judge who was hearing a case against a farmer who was in debt. Other farmers had dragged the judge from his courthouse and almost killed him.

By 1933 many American farmers were in a very serious position. Selling a wagon load of oats earned them less than the price of a pair of shoes. The price of many other crops was too low even to cover harvesting costs. Farmers were leaving them to rot in the fields.

During the Hundred Days, Roosevelt set up the Agricultural Adjustment Agency (AAA) to help the farmers. The AAA aimed to persuade farmers to produce less meat, corn, cotton and other main crops. The idea was to make such products scarcer, so that selling prices would rise and farmers would be better off. Farmers who agreed to grow less were given money by the government to make up for having less to sell.

To many people this seemed wicked. With millions of people hungry, the government was paying farmers *not* to grow food! But for the farmers this crop limitation scheme, as it was called, did its job. By 1936 they were earning half as much again as they had in 1933. By 1939 they were earning twice as much.

homeless. The Agricultural Adjustment Administration (AAA) set out to raise crop prices by paying farmers to produce less. The Tennessee Valley Authority (TVA) built a network of dams to make electricity and stop floods in a poor southeastern region of the United States. And the National Recovery Administration (NRA) worked to make sure that businesses paid fair wages and charged fair prices.

Workers on a W.P.A. project in the middle of the 1930s.

The American people knew both these and later New Deal organizations by their initials. Let us look more closely at the work of some of these "alphabet agencies."

Roosevelt believed that his most urgent task was to find people work. He was especially anxious about the young. Thousands were stealing rides on freight trains and wandering about the country searching for jobs. Roosevelt set up the CCC to help them. By August 1933, the CCC had already placed 250,000 young men in camps all over the country. They were hard at work cutting fire-lanes through forests, strengthening river banks against flooding, planting trees in places where the soil was being blown away. The government gave the CCC workers food and shelter and a wage of a dollar a day. Many sent this wage home to help their less fortunate relatives.

A later alphabet agency was the Works Progress Administration (WPA). Roosevelt set up the WPA in 1935. Like the CCC, it aimed to set people to work on jobs that were useful to the community. By 1937 its workers had built thousands of miles of new roads and thousands of schools and hospitals. The WPA even found work for unemployed writers and artists. The writers produced guidebooks to states and cities. The artists painted pictures on the walls of post offices and other public buildings.

Alphabet agencies like the CCC and the WPA put millions of people to work. Between 1935 and 1942 the WPA alone provided eight million jobs. This meant that people were able to support themselves once more. They regained their independence and self respect. This was not all. The money they were paid helped to bring trade back to life. Shops had customers again. Factories became busy once more. Farmers had someone to buy their produce.

This was what Roosevelt had hoped for. He believed that putting money into people's pockets was like pouring fuel into an engine that had stopped to make it start again. The engine could then once more drive the economic machinery that earned the country its living.

TVA – Democracy at work

The Tennessee is one of the great rivers of America. It drains an area of the eastern United States almost as large as West Germany. The valley of the Tennessee was once a country of tree-covered slopes, but generations of farmers cut down the trees and ploughed the slopes to grow corn, tobacco and cotton. All these crops were planted in the spring and harvested in the autumn. In the winter the land lay bare. Its soil was washed away by heavy winter rains. The same rains often caused floods which drove people from their homes.

By 1933 the Tennessee Valley's land was exhausted. It was producing poorer crops every year. The very names that the farmers gave to the countryside – Hard Labor Creek, Long Hungry Creek, Poorland Valley – showed how hopeless they were.

Roosevelt set up a special alphabet agency to organize help for the Tennessee Valley's millions of people. It was called the Tennessee Valley Authority (TVA). The TVA had three main aims – to stop floods, to make electricity and to make the land fertile again.

From 1933 onwards the valley of the Tennessee echoed to the roar of heavy machinery. Huge new steel and concrete dams rose up. When heavy rains fell the dams held back the flood water in great man-made lakes. By guiding the same water through turbines, they also made electricity. The TVA sold the electricity cheaply to farmers. The electricity was also used to power new factories making paper, aluminum, chemicals and fertilizers. These factories meant jobs and a better life for the Tennessee Valley's people.

TVA also planted millions of trees and persuaded farmers to plant crops like grass and clover. These covered the ground all year round and prevented winter rains from washing away the soil. The fields and hills of the Tennessee Valley became green again as the scars of erosion were healed.

Just as important as the achievements of TVA was the way in which they were won. In the 1930s the people of many countries were accepting the rule of dictators in a desperate attempt to escape from

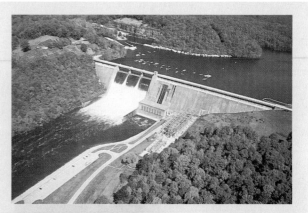

One of the dams built by the Tennessee Valley Authority.

the miseries of poverty and unemployment. In times like these the TVA was a startling demonstration of what democratic methods of government could achieve. Far from limiting the part people were able to play in running their own lives, as happened in the countries of the dictators, TVA encouraged them to take a more active part. It set up voluntary cooperative groups to sell electricity, for instance, and to organize the marketing of the farmers' produce. Such groups were run by the people themselves. They provided valuable experience of democracy at work at the local level – what has been called "democracy at the grass roots."

Roosevelt himself regarded this aspect of TVA as one of the most important things about it. In 1940 the armies of the German dictator Hitler seemed about to destroy the last remnants of democracy in Europe. That September, Roosevelt traveled to the Tennessee Valley to open a new dam. In his speech he pointed to the TVA as living proof of what the ideals and methods of democratic government could achieve:

"These fine changes we see have not come by compulsion. Thousands of townspeople have met together in the common effort. They have debated it and discussed it. No farmer was forced to join this movement. No workman was compelled to labor here for less than a rightful wage. No citizen has lost a single one of these human liberties that we prize so highly. This is a demonstration of what a democracy at work can do."

Roosevelt helped industrial workers in other ways. In 1935 he persuaded Congress to pass a law to protect their right to join labor unions. He hoped this would give workers a better chance to bargain with employers.

But some big employers – Henry Ford was one – hated labor unions. They dismissed any worker who joined one. Strikes and fighting broke out in industrial areas of the country as unions struggled to win recognition. To stop the trouble another union law was passed. This was called the Wagner Act, after the man who guided it through Congress. The Wagner Act gave every worker the right to join a union, and it set up a body called the National Labor Board to protect this right.

But despite New Deal reforms like these, millions of Americans still lived in fear. What if their jobs disappeared again? Would only a breadline stand between them and starvation once more? "No," Roosevelt told them. In 1935 he brought in a law called the Social Security Act. One part gave government pensions to people unable to provide for themselves – old people, widows and the blind, for example. Another part gave the United States its first system of unemployment insurance. The money to pay for these benefits came from special taxes paid by both workers and employers. The unemployment scheme did not cover all workers at first. But in later years more and more were protected by it.

Not all Americans supported Roosevelt's New Deal policies. Some said that the country could not afford the money that he was spending. Others said that much of the money was being wasted anyway. They feared, too, that Roosevelt's policies would make people idle and stop them standing on their own feet. "You can't make the world all planned and soft," complained one businessman. "The strongest and best survive – that's the law of nature after all."

But such criticisms made little difference to Roosevelt's popularity with the voters. To millions of Americans he was the man who had given them jobs and saved their homes and farms. In 1936 they re-elected him President by the largest majority of votes in the country's history. As one wit put it, "Everyone was against the New Deal but the voters." Thirty years later a New York taxi driver still remembered how many Americans felt about Roosevelt in those years. "Roosevelt?" he said in a

television interview. "He was God in this country." Even so, it was not Roosevelt's New Deal that ended unemployment in the United States. The German dictator, Adolf Hitler, did that.

By 1939, despite the New Deal, ten million American workers again had no jobs. Then, in September 1939, Hitler's armies marched into Poland. The Second World War began. The United States quickly became the main supplier of weapons to the countries fighting Hitler – what Roosevelt described as "the arsenal of democracy." American factories began working all day and all night. The number of people without jobs fell. In 1941 the United States joined the war itself and unemployment disappeared. President Roosevelt was now too busy to give attention to further reforms at home. "Old Dr. New Deal has to be replaced by Dr. Win-the-War," he said. His New Deal was over.

Roosevelt's efforts as "Dr. Win-the-War" wore him out. By 1945 he was a sick man. A few weeks before the end of the war, on the morning of April 12, he suffered a stroke. Within hours he was dead. His Vice President, Harry Truman, took over as President of the United States.

By this time nearly all Americans were better off than they had been in the dark days of the Depression. Some argued that this was due mainly to the coming of war. But many thought the main cause was the New Deal. People still argue about this. But there is no argument about the importance of the New Deal in other ways.

The New Deal altered Americans' ideas about the rightful work of their national government. Before the New Deal most thought of the government as a kind of policeman. It was there just to keep order, while factory owners and businessmen got on with making the country richer. The Depression weakened this belief. Roosevelt taught Americans to look to the government to see that everyone had a fair chance to obtain what he called "the good things of life." Many Americans still remember him with respect and affection.

THE ARSENAL OF DEMOCRACY

In the 1930s every year seemed to bring a new war, or threat of war, somewhere in the world. Leaders like the German dictator Hitler threatened and bullied. Nations built more tanks, warships and military aircraft. President Roosevelt spoke to the American people in 1937 about wars being fought in Spain and China. "Innocent peoples, innocent nations are being cruelly sacrificed to a greed for power and supremacy," he warned. "If these things come to pass [happen] in other parts of the world, let no one imagine that America will escape."

But Spain and China seemed far away. Most Americans ignored Roosevelt's warning. They believed that the best thing to do was to let foreigners solve their problems themselves. Isolationists felt this particularly strongly. These were people who believed that Americans should try to cut off, or "isolate," the United States from the problems of the outside world.

Isolationist ideas were very strong in Congress during the 1930s. It passed a number of laws called Neutrality Acts. These said that American citizens would not be allowed to sell military equipment, or lend money, to any nations at war. Even non-military supplies such as foodstuffs would be sold to warring countries only if they paid cash for them and collected them in their own ships.

Then, in 1939, war broke out in Europe. By the summer of 1940 Hitler's armies had overrun all of western Europe. Only Britain – exhausted and short of weapons – still defied them. With Hitler the master of Europe, and his ally, Japan, becoming ever stronger in Asia, Americans saw at last the dangerous position of the United States, sandwiched between the two.

Roosevelt had already persuaded Congress to approve the first peacetime military conscription in American history and to suspend the Neutrality Acts. Now he sent Britain all the military equipment that the United States could spare – rifles, guns, ships. Early in 1941 the British ran out of money. In March Roosevelt persuaded Congress to accept his Lend Lease Plan.

The Issei and the Nisei

In the early 1940s more than 100,000 people of Japanese descent lived in the United States. These Japanese Americans were either "Issei" – those born in Japan – or "Nisei" – American-born Japanese. Most lived in California, where they had worked hard and been successful. By 1941, for example, Issei were producing half of California's fruit and vegetables. Others became successful doctors, lawyers, and businessmen.

After the attack on Pearl Harbor white Americans began to see every Japanese American as a potential spy or saboteur. Both Issei and Nisei were threatened and treated badly. Shops refused to sell them food. Finally, in March 1942, the government sent soldiers to take them from their homes to be interned in prison camps called "relocation centers."

Most of the internment camps were in remote, desert areas of the country. Over 100,000 Japanese American men, women and children were kept in them for the rest of the war. In later years the American Civil Liberties Union called their internment "the worst single violation of the civil rights of American citizens in our history."

The internment of the Issei and the Nisei was more than unjust. All the evidence seems to show that it was unnecessary. Thousands of Nisei fought bravely in the American army. And not one Japanese American was convicted of an act of disloyalty to the United States during the whole of the war.

Lend Lease gave Roosevelt the right to supply military equipment and other goods to Britain without payment. He could do the same for any country whose defense he considered necessary to the safety of the United States. American guns, food and aircraft crossed the Atlantic Ocean in large quantities. They played a vital part in helping Britain to continue to fight against Hitler. When Hitler attacked

The Japanese attack on Pearl Harbor, Hawaii.

the Soviet Union in June 1941, Roosevelt used the Lend Lease scheme to send aid to the Russians, too.

Fighting was also taking place in Asia at this time. Japanese forces had invaded Manchuria in 1931 and China in 1937. In July 1941, they also occupied the French colony of Indochina. This alarmed the American government. It saw the growing power of Japan as a threat both to peace in Asia and to American trading interests. Ever since the 1937 attack on China the United States had been reducing its exports to Japan of goods that were useful in war – aircraft and chemicals, for example. Now, in July 1941, it stopped all shipments of oil.

Japan faced disaster. It imported 80 percent of its oil from the United States. Without this American oil its industries would be paralyzed. "Japan is like a fish in a pond from which the water is being drained away," a senior naval officer told Emperor Hirohito.

In October, General Hideki Tojo became Japan's Prime Minister. Tojo was well known for his belief that a sharp use of force was often the best way to solve disagreements. This had earned him a nickname – the Razor. There was plenty of oil in Southeast Asia. Tojo decided that Japan must seize

it – and must make it impossible for the Americans to use their Pacific battle fleet to stop them.

On December 7, 1941, Japanese warplanes roared in over Pearl Harbor, Hawaii, the American navy's main base in the Pacific Ocean. Their bombs and torpedoes sank or badly damaged eight American battleships, blew up hundreds of aircraft and killed over 2,000 men.

When the Pearl Harbor attack took place, the United States and Japan were still at peace. The United States declared war on December 8, 1941. Since Germany was Japan's ally, Hitler then declared war on the United States. The war in Europe and the war in Asia became one war. Britain, the Soviet Union and the United States (the Allies) were the main countries on one side. Germany and Japan (the Axis) were the main countries on the other.

The United States government organized the whole American economy towards winning the war. It placed controls on wages and prices, and introduced high income taxes. Gasoline and some foods were rationed. Factories stopped producing consumer goods such as automobiles and washing machines, and started making tanks, bombers and other war

Women training to build aircraft during the Second World War.

supplies. The government also spent a vast amount – two thousand million dollars – on a top-secret research scheme. The scheme was code-named the Manhattan Project. By 1945 scientists working on the scheme had produced and tested the world's first atomic bomb.

Allied war planners agreed to concentrate on defeating Germany first. In 1942 the Soviet Union was under heavy attack by the Germans. To help the Russians, American generals recommended an early invasion of German-occupied France. But Winston Churchill, the British Prime Minister, persuaded Roosevelt to attack the Germans first in the Mediterranean region. Combined American and British forces landed in North Africa in November 1942, and joined other British forces already fighting there. Together, the Allied armies defeated the German general Rommel's Afrika Korps. In 1943 they invaded Sicily and the mainland of Italy. After months of bitter fighting, on June 4, 1944. they freed Rome from German control.

Two days later, on June 6, Allied troops invaded Normandy in German-occupied France. Their Supreme Commander was the American general Eisenhower. The invasion was code-named Operation Overlord. The day it took place was referred to as D-Day – D for Deliverance. From early in the morning of D-Day hundreds of Allied landing craft emptied their loads of men and weapons on to the flat Normandy beaches. German soldiers fought hard to push the invaders into the sea. But they

failed. By the end of July Allied soldiers were racing across France. Paris was liberated on August 24 and by September Allied forces had crossed Germany's western border.

But the Germans were not yet beaten. In December 1944, they launched a last fierce attack in the Ardennes region of Belgium. They punched back the Allied front line in a bulge many miles deep. This gave the battle its name – the Battle of the Bulge. It was a month before the Allies could organize a counterattack and drive back the Germans.

The Battle of the Bulge proved to be the last German offensive of the Second World War. On April 25, 1945, British and American soldiers met advancing Soviet troops on the banks of the River Elbe in the middle of Germany. On April 30 Hitler shot himself. German soldiers everywhere laid down their weapons and on May 5, 1945, Germany surrendered.

In the Pacific Japanese armed forces won some striking early victories. In only a few months they overran Southeast Asia and the islands of the western Pacific. By the summer of 1942 they had conquered over 1.5 million square miles of land, rich in raw materials and inhabited by more than 100 million people. The conquered lands included the Philippines, where thousands of American troops were trapped and forced to surrender.

The Second World War in the Pacific.

106

Hiroshima 1945: right or wrong?

At fifteen minutes past eight on the morning of August 6, 1945, an American B29 bomber dropped an atomic bomb on the city of Hiroshima. Forty-five seconds later the bomb exploded in a blinding flash. A mushroom-shaped cloud climbed high into the sky above the city. Below, where Hiroshima had been, burned a ball of fire. It was 1,800 feet across and the temperature at its center was 100 million degrees. "The war's over!" shouted one of the bomber's crew. "My God," said another, "what have we done?"

President Truman ordered the atomic bomb to be used. He believed that using it saved lives by ending the war quickly. At the time, and since, people have argued fiercely about whether he was right. Some believe that he was. Without Hiroshima, they say, the Americans would have had to invade Japan to end the war. Many more people than died at Hiroshima and Nagasaki, both Japanese and American, would then have been killed. Other people do not accept this reasoning. They argue that the Japanese government was ready to surrender before the bombings. More than half a century after the destruction of Hiroshima, the argument still continues.

Japan's first setback came in May 1942. In the Battle of the Coral Sea, aircraft from American carriers drove back a big Japanese invasion fleet that was threatening Australia. In June the Japanese suffered an even worse defeat. Their main battle fleet attacked an important American base called Midway Island. Again American warplanes beat them off with heavy losses. In the Battle of Midway the Japanese lost four aircraft carriers and many of their best pilots.

By the beginning of 1943 the Americans and their Australian and British allies had agreed upon a long-term plan to defeat the Japanese. They decided on a three-pronged attack. From Australia one prong would push northwards towards Japan through the Philippines. From Hawaii another prong would strike westwards through the islands of the central Pacific. Finally, the two Pacific offensives would be supported by a drive through Burma into the lands that the Japanese had conquered in Southeast Asia.

By June 1943, the Pacific offensives had begun. American forces advanced towards Japan by "island hopping" – that is, they captured islands that were strategically important, but bypassed others. In the remainder of 1943 and throughout 1944, Allied forces fought their way closer to Japan itself. In June 1944, an enormous American task force won control of the important Mariana Islands. In October American troops returned to the Philippines and cut off Japan from its conquests in Southeast Asia.

By 1945 Japan was within range of air attacks. American bombers made devastating raids on its cities. In June the island of Okinawa, less than 375 miles from the Japanese coast, fell to the Americans. American troops prepared to invade Japan itself.

But the invasion never came. On July 16, 1945, Allied scientists at work on the Manhattan Project tested the world's first atomic bomb. Even they were shocked by the result. They had invented the most destructive weapon the world had ever seen. On August 6 an American bomber dropped an atomic bomb over the Japanese city of Hiroshima. A few days later, on August 9, a second atomic bomb was dropped on the city of Nagasaki. Both cities were devastated and nearly 200,000 civilians were killed. On August 14 the Japanese government surrendered. The Second World War was over.

Hiroshima, August 1945.

PROSPERITY AND PROBLEMS

Post-war prosperity: a Limousine in New York.

"The war?" the former Red Cross worker said to the interviewer. "The war was fun for America." A strange thing to say, you may think. But Americans were the only people in the world that the Second World War had made better off. Their homes had not been bombed or their land fought over. Busy wartime factories had given them good wages.

In the years that followed the war Americans became better off still. Between 1947 and 1971 the value of their wages in buying power – their "real incomes" as this is called – more than doubled. Americans bought more houses, cars, television sets, consumer goods of every kind. They became the most prosperous people the world had ever seen. As early as 1960, 55 percent of all families owned washing machines, 75 percent owned cars, 90 percent had television sets and nearly all had refrigerators.

During these years of prosperity the United States was led first by President Truman (1945–53), then by President Eisenhower (1953–61). In 1961 a new President called John F. Kennedy (1961–3) was elected.

Kennedy told the American people that they were facing a "new frontier," one with both opportunities and problems. One big problem in their own country was poverty. Although most Americans were well-off, millions of others were too poor to lead decent lives. Some were crowded together in city slums. Others lived in places like old coal-producing districts where the mines had closed.

Kennedy was a Democrat, as Roosevelt had been. He tried to help the poor with government money and food. He also wanted to help other groups who were

The McCarthy witch hunts

The late 1940s and the 1950s were anxious years for Americans. Despite their prosperity, they were worried by fears of war. The nation they feared was the Soviet Union.

Both President Truman and President Eisenhower believed that the Soviet Union's communist way of running a country was cruel and wrong. They made up their minds to stop it from spreading to other countries–to "contain" it. But "containment" was not enough for some Americans. They saw communism as a dangerous disease. They believed that it threatened both the freedom of individual Americans and the "capitalist" economic system of the United States. They wanted to destroy communism, not merely contain it.

In 1949 such people received two unpleasant surprises. The first was when communist rulers won control of China. The second was when the Soviet Union exploded an atomic bomb. Only the Americans had possessed atomic bombs until then.

A wave of fear swept across the United States. Many Americans started to see communist plots everywhere. When soldiers from communist North Korea invaded South Korea in June 1950, their fears became stronger still. Some even believed that the government itself was full of traitors plotting to betray the country to the Russians.

An ambitious and unscrupulous politician named Joseph McCarthy used these fears to win fame and power for himself. He started what came to be called a "witch hunt"–a search for people he could blame for the supposed threats to the United States. In the early 1950s McCarthy accused all kinds of people–government officials, scientists, famous entertainers–of secretly working for the Soviet Union. He never gave proof, but Americans were so full of fears about communism that many believed him. McCarthy ruined hundreds of innocent people. People grew afraid to give jobs or even to show friendship to anyone he accused. If they did, they risked being named as traitors themselves.

Then people began to doubt McCarthy. They watched him questioning "suspects" on television. They saw that he was a bully and a liar. By the mid 1950s McCarthy had lost his power. He went on making wild accusations, but nobody listened. In 1957 he died. But "McCarthyism" had done serious damage to the United States' reputation for justice and fair play.

A New York City slum.

John F. Kennedy and Lyndon B. Johnson.

not getting a fair deal, like black Americans. But before Kennedy could do all these things he was shot and killed. This happened while he was driving through the streets of Dallas in November 1963.

Lyndon B. Johnson (1963–9) took over from Kennedy as President. Johnson had been Kennedy's Vice President. He had spent years as a member of Congress, making political friends and winning influence there. He used this influence to speed up Kennedy's plans for reform. One of his first actions was to persuade Congress to pass Kennedy's plan to improve the position of American blacks. In 1964 this became law as the Civil Rights Act.

Johnson also promised the American people a "war on poverty." He set up systems of health care for the elderly (Medicare) and for the poor (Medicaid). He also increased federal aid to education. He said that he wanted to turn the United States into "the great society"–a country where everyone received fair and decent treatment.

But Johnson himself caused his plans to fail. In the later 1960s he involved the United States more and more deeply in war in Vietnam. The huge cost of the war forced Johnson to give up many of his plans for improvements. Riots and protests flared up all over the country–against the war, against poverty, against continuing racial injustice.

By 1968 the American people were bitterly divided. Many blamed Johnson for the country's problems. He became so unpopular that he decided not even to try to get re-elected. In 1969 he gave up the Presidency and retired.

Richard Nixon (1969–74) was elected to take Johnson's place as President. Nixon was a Republican. He was much less interested than Kennedy and Johnson in helping the poor. The government was paying out more than enough money on welfare schemes already, he said. He believed that people should overcome hardship by their own efforts.

In November 1972, the American people re-elected Nixon. The main reason for this was that by then he was close to getting the United States out of the hated war in Vietnam. A cease-fire was finally signed in January 1973. Arrangements were made for all American fighting men to come home. The American people felt a huge sense of relief.

The Watergate affair

On the night of June 17, 1972, police in Washington arrested five burglars. They caught the burglars inside the Democratic Party's national headquarters in the Watergate office building. Journalists on the *Washington Post* newspaper started to look into the burglary. They discovered that the burglars had been paid to steal information to discredit President Nixon's Democratic opponents.

In February 1973, the Senate set up a committee to look into the Watergate affair. Its meetings were broadcast live on television. Day by day viewers watched the committee uncover a network of lies and dishonesty at the very heart of the nation's government. Nixon vowed time and time again that he had known nothing about the Watergate break-in. But as the investigations went on, fewer and fewer people believed him. Many began to demand that he should be impeached for misusing his powers as President.

The end came in August 1974. A tape recording made in Nixon's office proved that he had known all about the Watergate affair. His impeachment and even imprisonment now seemed certain. To avoid this, Nixon resigned as President of the United States part way through his term of office–the first man ever to do so.

To many people at home and abroad the Watergate affair seemed to show clearly that the American political system had gone rotten. But it was parts of that very system–the newspapers, the law courts, the Congress–which brought the misdeeds of the President and his advisers to light. They showed that not even the highest in the land was above the law.

Ironically, it was Nixon himself who perhaps best summed up this aspect of the Watergate affair. Shortly before his resignation he said:

"Some people will say that Watergate demonstrates the bankruptcy of the American system. I believe precisely the opposite is true. Watergate represented a series of illegal acts. It was the system that brought these facts to life and that will bring those guilty to justice."

A cartoon that appeared in the British press during the Watergate affair. President Nixon has been stabbed by the quill pen of the Washington Post's *investigative journalists.*

It was Nixon's moment of greatest triumph. But soon he was in trouble. He was accused of being involved in an illegal plan to discredit his political opponents, called the "Watergate Affair." Congress threatened to put him on trial – "impeach" him – for misusing his powers. To avoid this, Nixon resigned as President.

Nixon was followed as President first by Gerald Ford (1974–7) and then by Jimmy Carter (1977–81). Neither Ford nor Carter won much success or popularity as President. One reason for this was that both found it difficult to control inflation. The United States now imported lots of oil. After an Arab–Israeli war in 1973 international oil prices rose steeply. These oil-price increases caused general inflation. By 1980 prices in the United States were rising by 13.5 percent a year and this was making life difficult for many people.

In 1980 Americans elected a President they hoped would make a better job of running the country. He was a former film actor named Ronald Reagan. Like Nixon, Reagan was a Republican. At home, he showed little sympathy for the poor. He said that he aimed to make Americans depend less on government help and more on self-help. Abroad,

Reagan was determined to make the United States stronger than its old rival, the Soviet Union. He spent many millions of dollars on developing powerful new missiles and on research into weapons to knock out enemy missiles from space.

Many people at home and abroad criticized Reagan. Some said that he was unfeeling. Others believed that he was incompetent. Still others called him a dangerous warmonger. But Reagan's policies – including the spending on weapons – helped more Americans to find jobs. Businessmen made bigger profits. Most Americans – all except the poorest of them – became better off. This helped to make Reagan popular. So did his relaxed and friendly manner, which came over well on television.

Reagan was popular for another reason, too. After the shame of Vietnam and Watergate his simple "stand on your own feet and act tough" policies made many Americans feel proud of their country again. In 1984 they re-elected him as President by one of the biggest majorities in American history. He was still popular, and for much the same reasons, when his second term as President ended in 1989.

BLACK AMERICANS

"How should we punish Hitler?" a reporter asked a young American black girl towards the end of the Second World War. "Paint him black and bring him over here," was her bitter reply. It was the result of being treated as a second-class human being – of being told no, you can't attend this school, have this job, live in this house, sit on this park bench. And the reason? Because your skin is black.

The official term for all this was segregation – that is, separating blacks from the rest of the community and refusing them many of the rights enjoyed by other people.

In 1940 ten million of the country's total black population of thirteen million still lived in the southern United States, most of them in great poverty. By 1970 the situation had changed. The country's total black population was now about twenty-four million and twelve million lived outside the South, most of them in big northern industrial cities. A mass migration had taken place. More than 4.5 million southern blacks had caught buses and trains to the North and to California.

The big attraction for the migrants was well-paid jobs in the factories of cities like Chicago, Pittsburgh and Detroit. But there was another. Taking the road north or west promised an escape not just from poverty, but from the miseries and humiliations of segregation which were a part of every southern black's daily life. As one black migrant wrote, "I don't care where so long as I go where a man is a man."

During the Second World War, segregation started to break down, at least outside the South. Black workers earned more money than ever before working alongside whites in the busy wartime factories. Black servicemen not only fought and died, but ate and slept alongside their white fellow countrymen. "One thing is certain," wrote an observer in 1946, "the days of treating negroes like sheep are done with [ended]."

The black struggle for equal treatment became known as the Civil Rights movement. An important legal turning point came in 1954. In a case called

Black Americans at war

In 1940 the American army had only two black officers. The navy had none. That September the United States began to draft young men into the armed forces. Before this, fewer than 4,000 blacks were serving in the American army. Most were in support units – digging ditches, loading and unloading ships and trucks, serving food. Many of the young black recruits objected to this. "We want to be soldiers, not servants," they said.

The entire black community supported the recruits. So did many whites, including Eleanor Roosevelt, the wife of the President. The system was changed. On December 1, 1941, the American army and air force opened all types of positions to qualified blacks. Six months later the navy and the marine corps did the same.

During the Second World War black combat units fought in both Europe and the Pacific. One black unit in particular won great admiration. This was the 332nd Fighter Group of the United States Army Air Force. In the skies above France and Germany its pilots destroyed 261 enemy aircraft and won a total of 904 medals for bravery. In March 1945, the whole group was awarded a Distinguished Unit Citation.

The 332nd Group came to symbolize the struggle of all blacks for equality. Its wartime achievements helped to end segregation in the American armed forces. In July 1948, President Truman ordered "equality of treatment and opportunity for all persons in the Armed Forces without regard to race, color, religion or national origin."

Brown v. *Topeka* the Supreme Court declared that segregated schools were illegal and ordered that black children should be allowed to attend any school as pupils. In September 1957, black children tried to enrol at the previously all white high school in Little Rock, Arkansas. An angry mob gathered to prevent them. President Eisenhower sent troops to enforce the Supreme Court decision of 1954 and the children

Black passengers choose their own seats on buses after the success of the Montgomery bus boycott.

were admitted. So began a long struggle for equal rights in education. It was still going on more than thirty years later.

Another landmark in the black struggle came on December 1, 1955. A black woman named Rosa Parks got on a bus in the strictly segregated southern city of Montgomery, Alabama. She took a seat towards the back of the bus, as blacks were supposed to do. But then white workers and shoppers filled up the front section of the bus and the driver ordered her to give up her seat. Mrs. Parks decided that she would not be treated in that way. She refused to move.

Mrs. Parks was arrested. But the black people of Montgomery supported her. The National Association for the Advancement of Colored People (NAACP) helped them to persuade a judge to release Mrs. Parks from jail. Then they started a campaign to end segregation on buses. Led by a young clergyman named Martin Luther King, they began to stop using, or "boycott," the city's bus services. The boycott went on for a year. Finally, in November 1956, the Supreme Court declared that segregation on public buses was unconstitutional. Montgomery's public transport system was desegregated.

The success of the Montgomery bus boycott encouraged blacks in other places to act together against segregation. They boycotted stores where black workers were refused jobs, refused to pay rent until landlords improved housing conditions, and held "sit-ins" in restaurants that would not serve black customers. They achieved many successes.

A climax of the Civil Rights movement came in 1963. On a hot August day 200,000 people, black and white, took part in a mass demonstration in Washington to demand full racial equality. In a moving and dramatic speech, Martin Luther King told millions of Americans watching their televisions all over the country:

"I have a dream that one day this nation will rise up and live out these truths that all men are created equal. I have a dream that one day on the red hills of Georgia the sons of former slaves and the sons of former slaveholders will be able to sit down together at the table of brotherhood. I have a dream that my four little children will one day live in a nation where they will not be judged by the color of their skin but by the content of their character."

Martin Luther King speaking at the Lincoln Memorial, August 1963.

113

By this time John Kennedy was President. He sympathized with the blacks and worked out a plan to ensure that all Americans, of any race, would receive equal treatment. Kennedy sent his scheme to Congress to be made into a law. He was murdered before this could happen, but his successor, Lyndon Johnson, made getting the law passed one of his first aims.

In 1964 the Civil Rights Act became the law of the land. Many Americans hoped that its passing would mark the beginning of a new age of racial harmony and friendship in the United States. They were disappointed. The racial difficulties of the United States were too deep-rooted to be solved by simple alterations in the law, or by demonstrations and marches. Changes were needed in human attitudes and in underlying economic conditions.

In the 1960s most American blacks were still worse housed, worse educated, and worse paid than other Americans. Some rejected with contempt the ideas of leaders like Martin Luther King that blacks and whites should learn to live together side by side in equality and friendship. "There are many of my poor, black, ignorant brothers preaching the ignorant and lying stuff that you should love your enemy," proclaimed the leader of a group called the Black Muslims. "What fool can love his enemy?"

The Black Muslims were only a minority. But other black Americans were becoming increasingly impatient at their lack of progress towards real equality – especially economic equality. In the hot summers of the mid 1960s this impatience boiled over into violence.

In August 1965, the streets of Watts, a black ghetto in Los Angeles, became a battlefield. For six days police and rioters fought among burning cars and buildings. A large area was burned out. Thirty-four people were killed and over a thousand were injured.

The Watts riot was followed by others – in Chicago, Detroit, New York, Washington. A government inquiry blamed lack of jobs for the riots. But many believed the causes went deeper. When one black leader was asked about the violence he replied, "If a man's standing on your toe and you've petitioned, begged, pleaded, done everything possible and he still won't move – you've got to push him off."

In April 1968, Martin Luther King was murdered.

The dream deferred

Langston Hughes is one of the best known American poets of the twentieth century. He was also black. The poem below was inspired by his experiences of life in Harlem, the black ghetto of New York. To Hughes it seemed that the people of Harlem's hopes of better treatment had been delayed – "deferred" – for too long.

What happens to a dream deferred?

Does it dry up
like a raisin in the sun?
Or fester like a sore –
And then run?
Does it stink like rotten meat?
Or crust and sugar over –
like a syrupy sweet?

Maybe it just sags
like a heavy load.

Or does it explode?

Langston Hughes

He was shot dead on the balcony of a motel in Memphis, Tennessee, by a white sniper. Many blacks now turned to the Black Power movement. Black Power taught that the only way for blacks to get justice was to fight for it.

But in the 1970s and 1980s most blacks decided that voting was a more effective way to improve their position. Their idea was to elect blacks to positions of power – as city councilors, as mayors of cities, as members of Congress. Jesse Jackson, a former assistant of Martin Luther King's, became the chief spokesman for this idea. "We need 10,000 blacks running for office [trying to get elected]," he told them. "Just run! Run! Run! If you run you might lose. If you don't run, you're guaranteed to lose."

By 1985 more than 5,000 of the 50,000 elected officials in the United States were black. This number included the mayors of such large cities as Los Angeles, Chicago, Philadelphia and Washington. In 1988 Jackson himself came close to being chosen as the Democratic Party's candidate in the Presidential election of that year. And whites, as well as blacks, voted for him.

114

But most black Americans continued to be less well placed in life than white Americans. In the late 1980s black unemployment was still higher than white unemployment. The average incomes of black Americans were still lower than those of whites. So were their standards of health and education. Even so, their position had improved greatly since the 1960s. Large parts of Martin Luther King's 1963 "dream" had come true. Blacks and whites studied side by side in schools and colleges. They worked side by side in all kinds of occupations. Increasing numbers lived side by side in the same districts. As King had dreamed, people seemed to be learning to judge each other more by the content of their characters than by the color of their skins.

(right) Jesse Jackson announcing his candidacy for the 1988 presidential election.

Black is beautiful

In the 1960s black Americans began taking new pride in their African ancestry. It became fashionable to take African names, to wear long African robes and short African jackets called "dasheks." Bushy African hairstyles became the fashion for black America and were even adopted by white youngsters. Before long the most frequently seen and heard slogan in America was the three words: "Black is beautiful."

The Dance Theater of Harlem.

But black pride and racial awareness showed itself in more than dress and appearance. Schools were set up to teach black children the history, languages and customs of their African ancestors. One of the most striking ventures was a ballet school founded by a young dancer named Arthur Mitchell. In Mitchell's school, youngsters from the streets of New York's Harlem learned to create new and exciting dances which combined the techniques of classical European ballet with the beat of African drums. Within a few years they had become internationally famous as the Dance Theater of Harlem, playing to full theaters all over the world.

Arthur Mitchell was a dancer, not a politician. His ways of trying to improve the position of his fellow blacks were very different from Martin Luther King's. Yet his underlying view of people, of their hopes and needs, was not so different. "I used to be full of anger," Mitchell told a reporter when the Dance Theater of Harlem visited London in 1976, "but not any more. Screams and yells don't get you anywhere. I discovered that black or white, green or purple, all kids are the same. People are the same. I don't think of myself as a black man, first and foremost. I'm just a man who happens to be black."

SUPERPOWER

—— 28 ——
COLD WAR AND KOREA

The United States was the strongest country on earth in 1945. Its factories produced half the world's manufactured goods. It had the world's biggest air force and navy. And it was the only nation armed with atomic bombs.

After the United States came the Soviet Union. Soviet soldiers were the masters of all Europe from the middle of Germany eastwards. After driving out Hitler's armies they had helped communists to take over the governments in country after country there. In 1946 Britain's wartime leader, Winston Churchill, spoke of an "Iron Curtain" across Europe, separating these communist-ruled nations of the east from the countries of the west.

The Americans and the Russians had fought Hitler's Germany together as allies. But friendship between them barely lasted the war out. The Russian dictator, Stalin, knew that many Americans hated the Soviet Union's communist way of life. He feared that the United States might drop atomic bombs on his country at any moment. The new American President, Truman, was just as suspicious of the Soviet Union. He suspected that Stalin's actions in eastern Europe were the first steps in a plan to convert the world to communism. The United States and the Soviet Union became deeply suspicious of one another. People began to speak of a "Cold War" between them. Although the two countries were not actually fighting, they were always quarreling.

Truman decided to use American power and money to "contain" Soviet influence – that is, to stop it from spreading. In 1947 he sent money and supplies to help the government of Greece to beat communist forces in a civil war. From this time on, containing communism became the main aim of the United States in dealing with the rest of the world. Because Truman started the policy, containment is sometimes called the Truman Doctrine.

The division of Germany

When the fighting in Europe ended in the spring of 1945, soldiers from the main Allied powers – the United States, the Soviet Union, Britain, and France – each occupied one of four zones into which Germany was divided. The idea was that this division would only be temporary. Once the Allies could agree on the details, they intended the whole country to be ruled again by one government. Each wanted to be sure, however, that this united Germany would be friendly towards them.

Stalin felt especially strongly about this. The Soviet Union had suffered from the Germans more than anyone. The only friendly Germany Stalin could think of was a Germany controlled by communists. The United States, Britain, and France were determined to prevent this. The result was that little progress was made in the many discussions that were held about Germany's future.

By 1946 it was already becoming clear that not one but two Germanies were beginning to take shape – a communist one in the Russian-controlled east of the country and a non-communist one in the west.

Deep inside the Russian zone was the city of Berlin. Since Berlin was Germany's old capital, it, too, had been divided between the Allies into areas called sectors. To link the western sectors of Berlin with the outside world the Russians had agreed to let goods and people pass freely through their zone of Germany.

Europe's recovery from the Second World War was painfully slow. By the summer of 1947 two years had passed since the last shots were fired. Yet millions of people were still without work, without decent homes, without sufficient food.

Allied leaders meet to divide up Europe at the Potsdam Conference, 1945.

In France and Italy communist parties won lots of support by promising reforms to make things better. This worried President Truman. In the summer of 1947 his government put forward a scheme that he hoped would help Europe's people and also make communism less appealing to them. The scheme was called the Marshall Plan, after General George Marshall, the Secretary of State who announced it.

The United States had plenty of all the things that Europe needed in 1947 – food, fuel, raw materials, machines. The trouble was that Europe was too poor to buy them. To solve this problem Marshall offered to give European countries the goods they needed. Marshall offered help to the Soviet Union, too. But a Soviet newspaper described his scheme as "a plan for interference in the home affairs of other countries." Stalin refused to have anything to do with it. He also made sure that none of the countries on the Soviet Union's side of the Iron Curtain accepted help either.

But millions of dollars' worth of American food, raw materials and machinery started to pour into western Europe. It was like giving a dying person a blood transfusion. By the time the Marshall Plan ended in 1952, western Europe was back on its feet and beginning to prosper.

By then containment was being tested in Asia also. The test was taking place in Korea. Before the Second World War, Korea had been ruled by Japan. When Japan surrendered in 1945, the north of Korea was occupied by Soviet forces and the south by Americans. The boundary between the two areas was the earth's 38th parallel of latitude.

Life in Nuremberg, Germany at the end of the Second World War.

117

Airlift to Berlin

By 1948 the Western Allies were eager to rebuild the German economy. Without German industrial production and German customers for their goods other European nations were finding it very difficult to revive their own economies. But before this problem could be solved, something had to be done about German money. In 1948 this was almost worthless. An ordinary factory worker then earned between 75 and 100 marks a week. *One* cigarette would have cost twenty-five marks.

In June 1948, the Western Allies announced that in their zones they were calling in all the old money and making a fresh start with new currency. The Russians were furious. Stalin's Foreign Minister, Molotov, had already attacked the Western plans to rebuild Germany's industries. Now he complained that the currency scheme was a plan "to convert western Germany into a base for extending the influence of American imperialism in Europe."

On June 24, 1948, a few days after the new money came into use, the Russians stopped all traffic between west Germany and west Berlin. To start with they may have intended simply to persuade the Western Allies to change their economic policies. But soon they became more ambitious. They blocked all the roads, railway lines and canals between Berlin and the western zones of Germany. Their aim now was to make it impossible for the Western Allies to supply the two million people living in their sectors of Berlin with sufficient food and fuel. They hoped that this would force the Western troops and officials to go, leaving the city to the Russians.

The leaders of the United States and Britain felt that they could not accept defeat in this matter.

Berliners greeting a U.S. plane during the Berlin airlift. of 1948–49.

They decided to send in everything Berlin needed by air. Fleets of American and British planes began to fly in supplies. This "airlift" went on for almost a year. On its busiest day nearly 14,000 aircraft landed on the city's airfields. Over two million tons of supplies were delivered, including a daily average of 5,000 tons of coal.

By the end of 1948 the Russians knew they were beaten. In February 1949, secret talks began and in May Stalin stopped the blockade.

The Berlin blockade finished all hope of uniting Germany under one government. In 1949 the Western Powers joined their zones together to form the Federal German Republic, or West Germany. Stalin replied by turning the Russian zone into the German Democratic Republic, or East Germany.

In 1948 the occupation of Korea ended. The Soviet army left behind a communist government in the north and the Americans set up a government friendly to themselves in the south. Both these governments claimed the right to rule all of the country. In June 1950, the North Koreans decided to settle the matter. Their soldiers crossed the 38th parallel in a full-scale invasion of South Korea.

President Truman sent American soldiers and warplanes from Japan to fight for the South Koreans. Then he persuaded the United Nations Organization, which had taken the place of the pre-war League of Nations, to support his action. Sixteen nations eventually sent troops to fight in the United Nations' forces in Korea. But the war was really an American affair. Nine out of every ten

U.N. soldiers in Korea were Americans. So, too, was their commander, General Douglas MacArthur.

At first the communist armies advanced easily. But after three months of hard fighting the Americans pushed them back across the 38th parallel and advanced deep into North Korea. By this time the American aim was no longer simply to protect South Korea. They wanted to unite all of Korea under a government friendly towards the United States.

Korea has a long border with China. Only a year earlier communists led by Mao Zedong had won a long struggle to rule China by driving out Chiang Kaishek. The Americans had backed Chiang in the struggle and in 1950 they still recognized him as China's rightful ruler. Mao feared that if all Korea came under American control they might let Chiang use it as a base from which to attack China.

Mao warned the Americans to stay back from China's borders. When his warning was ignored he sent thousands of Chinese soldiers to help the North Koreans. The Chinese drove back the advancing Americans. A new and fiercer war began in Korea. It was really between the United States and China, although neither country officially admitted this.

The Korean War dragged on for another two and a half years. It ended at last in July 1953. One reason it

South Korean women and children flee from the approaching North Korean army as U.S. troops advance to the battlefront.

The birth of NATO

In the years after 1945 the non-communist governments of Western Europe looked uneasily at the huge Russian armies grouped just behind the barbed-wire fences of the Iron Curtain. They feared that Stalin might order his soldiers to over-run them. In February 1948, their fears increased. With Russian support a communist government took control in Czechoslovakia. Then, in June, Stalin started the blockade of Berlin.

These events convinced President Truman that Western Europe needed more than economic aid. In 1949 he invited most of its nations to join the United States in setting up the North Atlantic Treaty Organization (NATO). This was an alliance of nations who agreed to support one another against threats from the Russians and set up combined armed forces to do this.

The North Atlantic Treaty was signed in Washington in April 1949. The following September Americans heard the news that the Russians, too, could now make atomic bombs. This persuaded Congress to vote millions of dollars to equip NATO's armed forces. In 1951 General Eisenhower, one of the United States' best known generals of the Second World War, was placed in command of these forces. Soon thousands of American soldiers were in Europe once more.

ended was the death of Stalin, who had been encouraging the Chinese to fight on. Another was the fact that the newly-elected President Eisenhower hinted that the Americans might use atomic weapons if the Chinese did not sign a cease-fire.

The cease-fire left Korea still divided more or less along the line of the 38th parallel. One Korean in every ten had been killed and millions made homeless. Yet both sides claimed that they had won a kind of victory. The Chinese said that they had proved that nobody need be afraid of opposing the Americans. The Americans said that they had shown communists everywhere that it did not pay to try to spread their rule by force. More than 33,000 Americans had died in Korea and over 100,000 more had been wounded. Containment in Asia had been expensive. But the Americans felt that it had worked.

29
A Balance of Terror

The H-bomb.

The bomb exploded in a blinding burst of green-white light. The fireball at its center grew into a towering pillar of flame. A huge, colored mushroom of poisonous cloud boiled high into the sky. It was November 1952. American scientists testing a new weapon had blasted a whole uninhabited island out of the Pacific Ocean. They had exploded the first hydrogen, or H-bomb.

The H-bomb was many times more destructive than the atomic, or A-bomb, that destroyed Hiroshima. Just one H-bomb had five times the destructive power of all the bombs dropped in five years of the Second World War. By 1953 the Russians, too, had made an H-bomb. By 1957 so had the British. But only the Americans and the Russians could afford to go on making them. The fact that both the United States and the Soviet Union had H-bombs determined how they behaved towards one another for years to come.

That same November of 1952 Dwight D. Eisenhower became President. American Presidents appoint a Secretary of State to take charge of the United States' dealings with foreign countries. Eisenhower gave this job to John Foster Dulles.

Dulles was a man of strong moral convictions. He genuinely believed that communism was evil. Truman, Dulles claimed, had not been tough enough with the Soviet Union. His own idea was for the United States to take the offensive. Instead of being content simply to contain communism ("a cringing policy of the fearful," as he called it) the United States should set out to "liberate" nations already under communist rule. In a broadcast in 1953 he told the peoples of eastern Europe that they could trust the United States to help them.

In 1956 the people of Hungary put Dulles's promise to the test. They had been under Soviet control since 1946. Now they rose in rebellion against their communist rulers. When Russian tanks rolled in to crush them they sent out desperate appeals for help. The help never came. Thousands of refugees fled across the Iron Curtain to safety in the neighboring country of Austria. "We can never believe the west again," one of them told a reporter.

Dulles failed to help the Hungarians because he knew that doing so would mean war with the Soviet Union. The devastation of nuclear war was, he decided, too high a price to pay for "rolling back" the Iron Curtain.

The way Dulles dealt with the Soviet Union in the later 1950s became known as "brinkmanship." This was because he seemed ready to take the United States to the brink – the edge – of war to contain communism. Dulles backed up his brinkmanship with threats of "massive retaliation." If the United States or any of its allies were attacked anywhere, he warned, the Americans would strike back. If

The Space Race

"I believe that this nation should commit itself to achieving the goal, before this decade is out, of landing a man on the moon and returning him safely to earth."

President Kennedy's proposal in May 1961 that the United States should send a man to the moon was eagerly welcomed by politicians and the American people. Soon work had begun on the Apollo program, as the project was named.

The Apollo program was another move in the "space race" between the United States and the Soviet Union. The costs of this race were enormous. But there were two important reasons why both the Americans and the Russians were willing to pay them. First, there was the question of international prestige – of gaining the respect of the rest of the world by achieving something calling for immense scientific and technical skill. Secondly, both Americans and Russians felt that to let the other side get too far ahead in space technology would endanger their security. Earth-orbiting satellites could be used to take spy photographs. More frightening still, rockets capable of carrying people into space could also be used to carry nuclear warheads.

Up to the mid-1960s each side matched the other's achievements in the space race. But then the Americans started to draw ahead. Finally, they were ready for the mission to put the first men on the moon – Apollo 11.

The Apollo 11 spacecraft was launched from Cape Canaveral on the coast of Florida. It carried three men as its crew – Neil Armstrong, Edward "Buzz" Aldrin and Michael Collins. The first two would

Neil Armstrong on the moon.

pilot the section of the spacecraft that would actually land on the moon's surface, the lunar module. Collins had the job of circling the moon in the other section of the spacecraft, the command module, waiting for their return.

The final countdown started five days before blast off. At last, on July 16, 1969, burning 4½ tons of fuel a second, a huge 5,000 ton rocket rose slowly from its launching pad on a roaring column of flame. Five days later millions of television viewers all over the world watched Armstrong and Aldrin step down on to the surface of the moon.

The two men spent three hours collecting rock samples and setting up scientific instruments on the moon's surface to send information back to earth after they left. Then they rejoined Collins in the command module. Three days later they splashed down safely in the Pacific Ocean and helicopters carried them off to a heroes' welcome.

necessary they would drop nuclear bombs on the Soviet Union and China. By the mid-1950s the United States had a powerful force of nuclear bombers ready to do this. On airfields all round the world giant American planes were constantly on the alert, ready to take off at a moment's notice.

Most Americans supported Dulles's massive retaliation policy at first. Then, on October 4, 1957, the Soviet Union sent into space the world's first

earth satellite, the Sputnik. Sputnik did not worry the Americans. But the rocket that carried it into space did. A rocket powerful enough to do that could also carry an H-bomb to its target.

The American government began to speed up work on rockets of its own. Soon it had a whole range of bomb-carrying rockets called "nuclear missiles." The biggest were the Inter-Continental Ballistic Missiles. These were kept in underground forts all over the United States, ready to carry their deadly warheads far into the Soviet Union. The Polaris, another missile, was carried by nuclear-powered submarines cruising deep beneath the oceans.

By the end of the 1950s the United States and the Soviet Union had enough nuclear missiles to kill everybody on earth. It is not surprising that people spoke of a "balance of terror." Both Russian and American leaders came to see that in a full-scale war between their two countries there could be no winner. They would simply destroy one another.

Nikita Khrushchev, the man who took Stalin's place as leader of the Soviet Union, realized this. He once said that capitalist and communist countries would only really agree "when shrimps learned to whistle." But in a world of H-bombs he believed that they had to try to live peacefully, side by side. In place of Cold War threats he suggested "peaceful coexistence."

President Eisenhower welcomed Khrushchev's talk of peaceful coexistence. He invited the Soviet leader to visit the United States. Afterwards the two men agreed to hold a summit meeting in Paris to work out solutions to some of their differences.

The Paris summit never even started. As the leaders were on their way there in May 1960, a Russian missile shot down an American aircraft over the Soviet Union. The aircraft was a U-2 spy plane, specially designed to take photographs of military targets from the edge of space. Krushchev angrily accused Eisenhower of planning for war while talking peace. He went angrily back to the Soviet Union. He seemed to be furious. But maybe he was rather pleased at having made the Americans look like hypocrites. In any case, the Paris summit meeting was over before it even started.

The Berlin Wall

Just after midnight on Sunday, August 13, 1961, trucks rolled through the silent streets of East Berlin. At the border with West Berlin soldiers jumped out and blocked the streets with coils of barbed wire. By morning they had closed off all but twelve of the eighty crossing points to West Berlin. Within days workmen were replacing the barbed wire with a lasting barrier of concrete. The Berlin Wall had been born.

To understand why the Berlin Wall was built we have to go back to the late 1940s. Since its formation in 1949 West Germany had prospered. By 1961 its people were among the best-off in the world. East Germans were less fortunate. Their wages were lower. They had less to buy in the shops, less chance to speak their minds. Millions fled to the West. The easiest way to do this was to catch a train from East to West Berlin and not bother to come back.

By July 1961, the number of East Germans making these one-way trips had risen to 10,000 a week. Many were highly skilled workers—engineers, doctors, scientists. East Germany's rulers knew that their country could never prosper

Berlin – the writing on the wall.

without such people. They built the Wall to stop any more from leaving.

President Kennedy was not prepared to risk war by demolishing the Berlin Wall. But he made it clear that the United States would not let the communists take over West Berlin.

For almost thirty years Berlin became two separate cities. It was not until 1989 that its people tore down the Wall as a first step towards re-uniting their city.

Crisis over Cuba

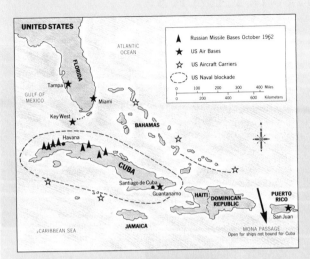

The Cuban Missile Crisis — the American blockade.

Cuba is an island nation only ninety miles from the coast of the United States. In 1959 a revolutionary reformer named Fidel Castro took over its government. Cuba's banks, railroads and many other businesses were owned by Americans at this time. So, too, were many of its big sugar plantations.

Castro needed money to make changes in Cuba. To obtain it he began to take over American-owned businesses. In the opinion of the United States government this was stealing American property. Not only this, but Castro seemed to be organizing a communist state right on the doorstep of the United States.

In 1960 President Eisenhower agreed to give weapons and ships to refugees from Cuba who wanted to overthrow Castro. When Eisenhower retired in January, 1961, the plan was supported also by the new President, John F. Kennedy.

On April 17, 1961, a force of 1,400 anti-Castro Cubans landed at the Bay of Pigs on Cuba's south coast. Castro had tanks and 20,000 men waiting. Within days the invaders were all captured or killed. But Castro believed that Kennedy would attack again, so he asked the Soviet Union for help. Khrushchev sent him shiploads of rifles,

tanks, and aircraft. Kennedy grew worried and ordered a close watch to be kept on Cuba.

On Sunday, October 14, 1962, an American U-2 spy plane flew high over the island taking photographs. They showed Russian missile launching sites being built. What had happened was this: Ever since the U-2 incident of 1960 Khrushchev had been making threats against the United States. These had alarmed Kennedy. Although the Americans already had more long-range missiles than the Russians, Kennedy ordered nearly a thousand more. The new missiles tipped the "balance of terror" strongly in favor of the United States. When Castro asked for help, Khrushchev saw a chance to level up the balance of terror. He would threaten the United States from missile bases on its own doorstep — Cuba.

Kennedy was shocked by the U-2 photographs. "This is the week I better earn my salary," he said grimly. Some advisers wanted him to send bombers to destroy the missile bases. He also thought about sending American soldiers to capture them. But instead he ordered American ships and aircraft to set up a blockade. They were to stop any Soviet ships carrying more missile equipment to Cuba.

Kennedy then told Khrushchev to take away the Soviet missiles and destroy the bases. He warned that any missile fired from Cuba would be treated as a direct Soviet attack on the United States and ordered 156 long-range missiles aimed at the Soviet Union to be made ready to fire.

For ten terrifying days in October 1962, the world trembled on the edge of nuclear war. People waited in fear for the next news flash on their radios and televisions. Finally Khrushchev ordered his technicians in Cuba to destroy the launching sites and return the missiles to the Soviet Union. In return, Kennedy called off the blockade and promised to leave Cuba alone. Privately, he also agreed to remove American missiles sited on the border of the Soviet Union in Turkey. The most dangerous crisis of the Cold War was over.

THE VIETNAM YEARS

The Vietnam Memorial, Washington D.C.

One of the landmarks of Washington, D.C., is a massive building of white marble. It is a memorial to Abraham Lincoln. Close by, almost hidden in a hollow in the ground, stands another memorial. This memorial is not to one man but to many. It is a long wall of polished black marble and on it are carved many thousands of names. The names are those of young Americans who died in the Vietnam War.

Vietnam is in Southeast Asia. Once it was ruled by France. But in 1954 the French were driven out by the soldiers of a communist leader named Ho Chi Minh. Like Korea, Vietnam was then divided in two. Communists ruled the North and non-communists the South.

The next step was supposed to be the election of one government for the whole country. But the election never took place—mainly because the government of South Vietnam feared that Ho Chi Minh and his communists would win. Ho Chi Minh set out to unite Vietnam by war. He ordered sabotage and terrorism against South Vietnam. As part of their worldwide plan to contain communism, the Americans had already helped the French against Ho. Now they sent weapons and advisers to the government of South Vietnam.

Containment was especially important to the Americans in Vietnam. This was because of an idea that President Eisenhower called the "domino theory." The domino theory went like this: Asia has a lot of unsettled countries. If one of them – Vietnam, say – fell under communist rule, others would follow. They would be knocked over one by one, like a line of falling dominoes.

Americans were especially afraid that communist China might try to take control in Southeast Asia as the Soviet Union had done in eastern Europe. So, in the 1950s and early 1960s, first President Eisenhower and then President Kennedy poured American money and weapons into South Vietnam. Kennedy sent soldiers, too – not to fight, themselves, but to advise and train the South Vietnamese forces.

By the early 1960s, however, it was clear that the government of South Vietnam was losing the war. Ho Chi Minh had a guerilla army of 100,000 men fighting in South Vietnam by then. These guerillas were called the Vietcong. Many were communists from the North who had marched into the South along secret jungle trails. By 1965 the Vietcong controlled large areas of South Vietnam. The country's American-backed government was close to collapse.

By now the United States had a new leader, President Lyndon B. Johnson. Johnson faced a difficult choice. He could leave Vietnam and let the communists take over, or he could send in American soldiers to try to stop them. Johnson was too worried about the domino theory – and too proud – to make the first choice. He had already ordered American aircraft to bomb railways and bridges in North Vietnam. Now he sent in American soldiers. By 1968 over 500,000 were fighting in South Vietnam. The Russians and the Chinese sent more weapons and supplies to Ho Chi Minh. Thousands more of his communist troops marched south to do battle with the Americans.

The Vietnam War was one of ambushes and sudden attacks. After an attack the Vietcong would melt away in the jungle, or turn into peaceful villagers. Ordinary villagers helped and protected the Vietcong. Sometimes they did this out of fear, sometimes out of sympathy. "The people are the water, our armies are the fish," one Vietcong leader said.

A guerilla war like this meant that the Americans often had no enemy to strike back at. As one soldier put it, to find the Vietcong was "like trying to identify tears in a bucket of water."

North Vietnamese soldiers.

American fighting men grew angry and frustrated. They sprayed vast areas of countryside with deadly chemicals to destroy the Vietcong's supply trails. They burned down villages which were suspected of sheltering Vietcong soldiers. But the fighting went on. It continued even when Johnson stepped up or "escalated" the war by bombing cities in North Vietnam to try to force the communists to make peace.

Film reports of the suffering in Vietnam were shown all over the world on television. For the first time in history people far away from any fighting were able to see in their own homes the horror and cruelty of modern war. Millions began to believe that the Americans were cruel and bullying monsters.

The war caused bitter disagreements in the United States. Countless families lost sons, brothers, and husbands in Vietnam. By the end of the 1960s many Americans were sick and ashamed of the killing and the destruction. "L.B.J., L.B.J., how many kids have you killed today?" shouted angry demonstrators.

President Johnson saw that by sending American soldiers to fight in Vietnam he had led the United States into a trap. The war was destroying his country's good name in the world and setting its people against one another. In 1968 he stopped the bombing of North Vietnam and started to look for ways of making peace.

In 1969 Richard Nixon was elected to replace Johnson as President. Like Johnson, he wanted to end the Vietnam War. But he, too, wanted to do so without the Americans looking as if they had been beaten.

Death at Kent State

Kent State University is in Ohio. In 1970, after riots there in protest against the war in Vietnam, any further demonstrations were banned. When a group of about 1,000 students defied the ban, they were fired on by soldiers. A ten-second burst of rifle fire killed four students and wounded another ten.

The Kent State tragedy showed how deeply the Vietnam War was dividing the American people. "After all, bullets against a gang of unarmed kids," said a student. "Too much, man, too much!" But when another student asked a passer-by why he was holding up his hand with four fingers extended, he was told that it meant "This time we got four of you bastards; next time we'll get more." "The volley of gunfire served its purpose," said a writer to a local newspaper. "It broke up a riot and I say the same method should be used again and again."

But most Americans were shocked by the killings and many were ashamed. They agreed with the father of one of the dead students, a girl named Allison Krause, when he asked bitterly, "Have we come to such a state in this country that a young girl has to be shot because she disagrees deeply with the actions of her government?"

Protesting against the Vietnam War in Washington D.C.

Bob Dylan

Songs of protest have played a part in American life for many years. These have been songs about the concerns of farmers, miners, cowboys, union members. All have had a common purpose – to express and to relieve people's feelings on subjects that are important to them. Their writers and performers have sometimes hoped that the songs might even help to change people's attitudes.

In the 1960s a young writer and singer named Bob Dylan used protest songs to support the anti-war movement of the time. By the 1970s Dylan had become a very popular – and very rich – international entertainer. But in the 1960s he was more than this. For many young people he was the voice of the conscience of their generation. His lyrics, often set to old tunes, were ironic comments on what he saw as the deceit and hypocrisy of those who held power. These verses from his song *With God on Our Side* are typical:

Oh, the history books tell it,
They tell it so well,
The cavalries charged,
The Indians fell.
The cavalries charged,
The Indians died,
Oh the country was young
With God on its side.

Oh, the First World War, boys,
It came and it went,
The reason for fighting
I never did get.
But I learned to accept it,
Accept it with pride,
For you don't count the dead
When God's on your side.

I've learned to hate Russians
All through my whole life,
If another war starts
It's them we must fight.
To hate them and fear them,
To run and to hide,
And accept it all bravely
With God on my side.

But now we got weapons
Of the chemical dust,
If fire them we're forced to
Then fire them we must.
One push of the button
And a shot the world wide,
And you never ask questions
When God's on your side.

Reproduced by kind permission of
Warner/Chappell Music, Inc.

Nixon worked out a plan to achieve this. He called it the "Vietnamization" of the war. He set out to strengthen the South Vietnamese army to make it seem strong enough to defend South Vietnam without help. This gave him an excuse to start withdrawing American fighting men from Vietnam.

Nixon then sent Henry Kissinger, his adviser on foreign affairs, to secret talks with North Vietnamese and Russian leaders in Moscow. In return for a cease-fire he offered to withdraw all American troops from Vietnam within six months. When the North Vietnamese were slow to agree he started bombing their cities again in order to "persuade" them. A sort of agreement was finally put together in January 1973. By March 1973, the last American soldiers had left Vietnam.

But the real end of the Vietnam War came in May 1975. As frightened Vietnamese supporters of the Americans scrambled for the last places on rescue helicopters, victorious communist tanks rolled into Saigon, the capital city of South Vietnam. The communists marked their victory by given Saigon a new name. They called it Ho Chi Minh City.

In Korea, twenty years earlier, the Americans had claimed that they had made containment work. In Vietnam they knew, and so did everyone else, that they had failed.

AMERICA'S BACK YARD

"Muera Nixon, Muera Nixon!" – Death to Nixon!

A barricade blocked the road. The car rocked wildly as the chanting mob tried to overturn it. Rocks and iron bars thudded against its roof and shattered its windows. Inside the car Richard Nixon, Vice President of the United States, was in great danger.

It was May 13, 1958, in Caracas, the capital of Venezuela. Nixon was visiting the city as part of a goodwill tour of Latin America. But he found only hatred on the streets of Caracas. Nixon's life was saved when a truck forced a way through the barricade and his car was able to accelerate away. When news of the attack reached the United States the American people were shocked and angry. But it made them realize how much some Latin Americans hated and resented their country.

American culture invades Mexico.

Latin America is the name given to the mainly Spanish-speaking countries which lie to the south of the United States. Ever since the early nineteenth century the United States has taken a special interest in what happens in these countries. They are its closest neighbors and so it is important to the safety of the United States to make sure that no foreign enemies gain influence in them.

In the past this has often meant that the rulers of these Latin American countries have been little more than American puppets. Their agriculture and industry have frequently been American-controlled, too. A classic example was Cuba. Up to the 1950s its railroads, banks, electricity industry and many of its biggest farms were all American-owned.

In 1933 President Franklin Roosevelt promised that the United States would respect the right of Latin American countries to control their own affairs. He called this the "good neighbor" policy. "I would dedicate this nation to the policy of the good neighbor," he said, "the neighbor who respects the rights of others."

Roosevelt ordered home the American soldiers and officials who had been running the affairs of Latin American countries at one time or another for much of the past thirty years. Nicaragua, for example, had been occupied by American troops from 1912 to 1933. He also gave up the United States' claim to interfere in Panama and Cuba whenever it wanted.

But many Latin Americans were not convinced by Roosevelt's talk about being a good neighbor. True, the American troops had gone home. But the rulers who took over when the soldiers left – the Somoza family, who held power in Nicaragua from 1937 to 1979, for example – usually did what the Americans expected of them.

The Second World War brought better times for Latin America. All the raw materials that it could produce – copper, tin, oil and countless others – were used by the wartime factories of the United States. The result was more money and more jobs – but also even more American control.

Reagan and the Sandinistas

Nicaragua is a country in Central America. In the 1970s it was ruled by a right-wing dictator named Somoza, who had close ties with the United States. Left-wing rebels organized a guerilla army to fight Somoza. The rebels called themselves Sandinistas, after a guerilla leader named César Augusto Sandino, who had fought against the American occupation of Nicaragua during the 1920s and 1930s.

The Sandinistas were supported by peasants, workers, priests and many business people. In 1979 they drove Somoza from the country and set up a new government. They promised the people of Nicaragua land reform, social justice and democratic government.

A poster in Managua, Nicaragua proclaims that Reagan is on his way out, but the revolution is here to stay.

At first the United States government welcomed the Sandinistas. President Carter offered them economic aid. But when Ronald Reagan became President in 1981 this policy changed.

Reagan believed that the Sandinistas were under the influence of the Soviet Union and Cuba. Soon he was describing their government as a communist dictatorship. Its aim, he said, was to spread revolution to other parts of Central America and he gave money and weapons to rebels who were trying to overthrow it. Most people called the rebels "contras" from the Spanish word for "counter-revolutionaries." President Reagan, however, called them "freedom fighters."

Many Americans criticized Reagan's policies. They warned that his enmity was forcing the Sandinistas into the arms of the Soviet Union. Other Americans supported the President. They believed that the safety of the United States depended on stopping Sandinista ideas from spreading to other nearby countries.

In February 1990 an election was held in Nicaragua. When the Sandinistas lost, they handed over power to a new government whose leaders were more acceptable to the United States and hopes for peace increased.

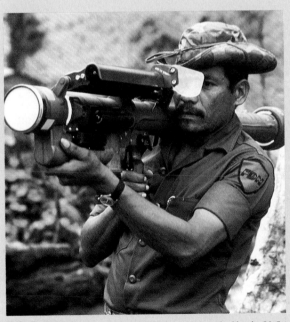

A Nicaraguan Contra rebel with Redeye missile supplied by the U.S.

As soon as the war ended fresh calls of "Yankee, go home" were heard. To try to reduce anti-American feeling, in 1945 the United States took the lead in setting up the Organization of American States (OAS). The idea of the OAS was to encourage the countries of Latin America to cooperate with one another, and with the United States, as partners. One of its aims was to improve living standards.

But hardship and hunger continued to be widespread in Latin America. In most countries there, extremes of poverty for the many and wealth for the few existed side by side. Oppressive governments controlled by the rich and backed by soldiers did little to improve the lives of the people.

American Hispanics

In 1950 the population of the United States included fewer than four million resident "Hispanics"—that is, people originating from Spanish-speaking countries. By the mid 1980s this number had increased to 17.6 million and was still rising fast. In some parts of the United States, especially in the South and West, it became more common to hear Spanish being spoken on the streets than English.

Illegal immigrants caught by U.S. border officials.

About 60 percent of the United States' resident Hispanics came originally from Mexico. The remainder came from other Latin American countries, such as Cuba and Colombia. The newcomers' usual reasons for coming were the same as those of earlier immigrants from Europe—to escape from poverty or political persecution in their homelands.

The increase in the number of Hispanics was partly the result of an important change in the American immigration system. The old immigration laws, which dated back to the 1920s, had favored Europeans. But in 1965 a new law said that what would count in the future was who applied first.

The result was a big increase in immigration from non-European countries. By the 1980s the United States was officially accepting 270,000 newcomers a year. Forty percent of these were coming from Asia and another forty percent from Latin America.

Many other immigrants entered the United States without permission. In 1985 the government estimated that the country had between two and ten million of these illegal immigrants, half a million of whom had arrived in the previous year. Many were Hispanics, who had waded across the shallow Rio Grande River that formed the border between the United States and Mexico. For obvious reasons, people who entered the United States in this way were called "wetbacks."

Reformers accused the United States of helping to keep these groups of wealthy tyrants in power. There was some truth in this. The American government often seemed more concerned with suppressing communism in Latin America than with improving conditions of life there. In 1954, for example, the American secret service (the Central Intelligence Agency, or CIA) encouraged the overthrow of a reforming government in Guatemala. When Guatemala's deposed President asked the United Nations to look into this, the Americans used their Security Council veto to prevent an investigation.

In later years American governments went on interfering in Latin American affairs. Sometimes they interfered openly, sometimes in more secret ways. In 1965 President Johnson sent 22,000 American marines to the Dominican Republic to stop a leader he distrusted from regaining power. In 1973 CIA agents helped generals in Chile to overthrow President Allende. Allende was sympathetic towards communist ideas and had nationalized some American-owned mining companies.

Actions like these help to explain why many Latin Americans continued to dislike their North

American neighbor. All over Latin America, it seemed, the United States was propping up oppressive and unpopular governments.

This was not the whole truth, of course. American dealings with Latin America had a more positive and humanitarian side. During their earlier occupations of countries such as Cuba and Nicaragua the Americans had built hospitals, supplied towns with pure water and wiped out killer diseases like malaria and yellow fever. In the early 1960s President Kennedy continued this tradition.

In 1961 Kennedy set up an organization called the Alliance for Progress. The United States gave millions of dollars to improve the lives of Latin America's poor. The money was used to build roads, homes and schools, and to improve water-supply and sanitation systems. The Alliance also advanced money to peasant farmers, so that they could buy more land. Kennedy hoped that aiding Latin America like this would enable governments there to make enough improvements to stop people from turning to communism.

But the generals running much of Latin America continued to rely more on guns than on reforms to keep power. Despite the generosity of schemes like the Alliance for Progress, many people saw little basic difference between the attitude of the United States towards Latin America and the attitude of the Soviet Union towards eastern Europe. In one way or another, both superpowers seemed determined to protect their own interests by controlling their smaller neighbors.

Kennedy's Peace Corps

In their rivalry with the Soviet Union, American governments never forgot the lesson of the Marshall Plan. They knew that communism is often most attractive to the people of countries where food is short and life is hard. From the 1950s onwards, therefore, they spent millions of dollars on modernizing farms, constructing power stations and building roads in countries as far apart as Turkey and Colombia, Pakistan and Chile. The idea of this "foreign aid" was to give poor people all over the world better lives, partly out of a genuine desire to help them but partly also to win new friends and supporters for the United States.

Foreign aid did not always take the shape of food, machines or money. Sometimes human skills were sent, in the form of teachers and technical experts. Soon after John F. Kennedy became President he started a new scheme of this kind when he set up an organization called the Peace Corps.

The idea of the Peace Corps was to use the enthusiasm and the skills of young Americans to help the people of "underdeveloped" – that is poor – nations to help themselves. All members of the Peace Corps were volunteers, who agreed to work for two years in the poor countries of Asia, Africa and Latin America.

Some Americans disliked the scheme. They said that the idea of sending immature young Americans to show the people of distant lands how to live was both naive and arrogant. But others thought the scheme worthwhile and exciting. "These kids represent something many of us thought had disappeared from America," said a New York psychologist, "– the old frontier spirit."

Whoever was right, the Peace Corps achieved at least one thing – for a while it gave a human face to the bare financial statistics of American foreign aid.

Young U.S. volunteers building a clinic in Lima, Peru.

AN END TO COLD WAR?

"They talk about who lost and who won. Human reason won. Mankind won." These words were spoken by the Soviet leader, Khrushchev, after the Cuban Missile Crisis of 1962. President Kennedy felt the same. Both men knew that for ten days they had been close to bringing death to millions of people. They began working harder to make such dangerous situations less likely.

In August 1963, the United States and the Soviet Union signed a treaty agreeing to stop testing new nuclear weapons in the atmosphere or under water. They also set up a special telephone link between Washington and Moscow. On this "hotline" American and Soviet leaders could talk directly to one another. In future any dangerous crisis would be dealt with more quickly and with less risk of misunderstanding.

The hotline proved its value in 1967. War broke out between Israel and Egypt. The United States was friendly with Israel, and the Soviet Union with Egypt. But both took great care not to let these friendships drag them into fighting one another.

By then Kennedy was dead and Khrushchev had been removed from power. But new American and Russian leaders went on trying to reduce tension. Even the long and bloody war in Vietnam was not allowed to interfere with "détente," as these moves were called.

President Nixon greeting Moscow citizens during his visit to the Soviet Union, 1972.

The Chinese communist leader, Mao Zedong, attacked détente. He accused Soviet leaders of "revisionism" – that is, of altering some of communism's most important ideas. He declared that the only way to deal with American capitalism was to be ready to fight it to the death. But a lot of the arguing about whether Russians or Chinese were the best communists was just a smoke-screen hiding the real quarrel between them, which was about land. The Chinese claimed that almost one million square miles of the Soviet Union were rightfully theirs. Big armies watched and sometimes fought on the long frontier between the two countries.

The enmity between China and the Soviet Union had important effects on both countries' relations with the United States in the early 1970s. Détente between the Soviet Union and the United States went on. And détente between the United States and China began.

In May 1972, President Nixon flew to Moscow to sign the Strategic Arms Limitation Treaty (SALT) with the Russians. The idea of SALT was to slow down the arms race. It was intended to save both countries money as well as to make war between them less likely. Each agreed how many missiles of various types the other should have, how many submarines to fire them from, and so on.

The first sign that China, too, was interested in détente with the United States came in 1970. For years the Chinese government had made it very difficult for anyone from western countries to visit China. But in 1970 it invited an American table-tennis team to play there. The American government, correctly, took this as a hint that the Chinese wanted to settle some of their differences with the United States.

The man behind the Chinese move was Zhou Enlai, China's Prime Minister. Zhou believed that China needed friends on the international scene, especially while the Soviet Union was so unfriendly. He persuaded Mao Zedong to try to end the twenty-year-old feud with the United States.

President Nixon's adviser, Henry Kissinger, flew to China for secret meetings with Zhou. Late in 1971 the United States agreed to communist China joining the United Nations, something it had vetoed for

President Nixon with Zhou Enlai in China, 1972.

years. In February 1972, Nixon flew to China to meet Mao. Mao was still suspicious of the Americans. But in the years that followed China and the United States made important agreements on trade and other matters, especially after Mao's death in 1976.

As China and the United States became more friendly, tension grew again between Russians and Americans. Russians still feared that the United States wanted to wipe out communism. Americans still feared that the Soviet Union wanted to conquer the world. American fears grew stronger when Russian soldiers marched into the Soviet Union's neighbor, Afghanistan, in December 1979. Because of the Soviet action, Congress refused to renew the SALT agreement.

Both the Soviet Union and the United States had continued to develop new and more deadly nuclear missiles during the years of détente. Attempts were made to slow down this arms race. But neither side would stop while it felt that the other was ahead. In the early 1980s, détente looked dead.

Henry Kissinger

In 1938 a fifteen-year-old Jewish boy was forced to flee from Germany with his parents in order to escape imprisonment in one of Hitler's concentration camps. The family went to live in the United States where the boy got a job cleaning bristles in a shaving-brush factory. He was clever and hardworking, however, and went on to become a brilliant student at Harvard University. Just over thirty years later he became the Secretary of State of the United States. His name was Henry Kissinger.

Kissinger's rise to importance began when Richard Nixon became President in 1969. He became Nixon's personal adviser in all the United States' dealings with the rest of the world. In 1973 Kissinger officially became Secretary of State, a position he held until Jimmy Carter became President in 1977.

All through the early and middle 1970s Kissinger played a central part in shaping American foreign policy. He helped to form and direct the Nixon government's policy in the later years of the Vietnam War. He prepared the way for détente with communist China. He worked to bring peace between the United States' ally Israel and its Arab neighbors.

Some people believed that Kissinger's boyhood experiences in Germany played an important part in forming his ideas about the kind of world he wanted to shape as Secretary of State. One man who knew him said:

Henry Kissinger, the man who shaped and directed American foreign policy for much of the 1970s.

"I think he came out of it with a kind of burning need for order. People in these experiences have a real memory of chaos, of violence and brutality, like the world is collapsing under them. Kissinger, more than most, would probably agree that disorder is worse than injustice."

Kissinger's critics saw him as a showman, whose achievements were more apparent than real. His admirers believed that he was one of the most effective statesmen of the twentieth century.

By the middle of the 1980s President Reagan had increased American military strength so much that he was ready to start talking seriously about slowing down the arms race. The Soviet Union was ready, too. In 1985 a new leader, Mikhail Gorbachev, had come to power there. Gorbachev believed that the huge cost of the arms race was crippling the Soviet Union's economy and he was eager to reduce it. In December 1987, Gorbachev traveled with his wife to the United States. There, in Washington, he and President Reagan signed the Intermediate Range Nuclear Force (INF) treaty.

In the INF treaty both countries agreed that within three years they would destroy all their land-based medium and shorter range nuclear missiles. President Reagan gave Gorbachev a pair of cufflinks to celebrate the signing of the treaty. To symbolize their two countries turning away from war and towards peace, the cufflinks showed swords being beaten into ploughshares.

In May 1988, Gorbachev began to withdraw Soviet troops from Afghanistan. The following year brought even bigger changes. All over central and eastern Europe the communist political systems imposed by Stalin in the years after the Second World War crumbled away. While Gorbachev's Soviet Union looked on without interfering, countries such as Hungary, Poland, East Germany, and Czechoslovakia set up multi-party systems and held free elections.

Such developments raised hopes that a new time of peaceful cooperation might now be possible between the Soviet Union and the United States. "I believe that future generations will look back to this time and see it as a turning point in world history," the British Prime Minister Margaret Thatcher had said after a visit to Washington in 1988. "We are not in a cold war now."

By 1990 most people believed that she was right.

Soviet leader, Mikhail Gorbachev, showing President Reagan Red Square during his visit to Moscow, 1988.

THE AMERICAN CENTURY

Denims and hot dogs, skyscrapers and supermarkets, mass production and rock music – what do all these have in common? One thing is that they can be found today all over the world. Another is that all of them were born in the United States. The country which for most of its existence had been an importer of influences has become in the twentieth century a major exporter of them. In many areas of life, American popular tastes and attitudes have conquered the world.

You have read earlier about the part that American movies played in this process. After the Second World War the spreading of American influence was continued by a powerful new force – television. As early as 1947, around 170,000 American families had television sets flickering in their living rooms. Thousands more were waiting for sets to be delivered. Soon millions of people were organizing their activities around the programs on television that evening.

Television.

Most early American television programs were concerned with entertainment. Comedy and game shows, stories about policemen and detectives, the adventures of fictional western heroes like the Lone Ranger – all these were very popular. The main purpose of such programs was to attract large audiences of "viewers." Manufacturing firms then paid television companies like NBC and CBS lots of money to show advertisements for their products while the programs were being broadcast, or "televised."

By the 1960s filmed television programs had become an important American export. Other countries found it cheaper to buy American programs than to make their own. Soon such exported programs were being watched by viewers all over the world. One of the most popular was "I Love Lucy," a 1950s comedy series featuring a red-haired comedienne named Lucille Ball. When Lucille Ball died in April 1989, "I Love Lucy" was still being televised. It had been seen by then in seventy-nine different countries and had become the most watched television show ever.

In music, the process of Americanization could be seen most clearly in the huge international popularity of rock. Rock began as "rock-and-roll", a music that was first played in the 1950s. It came from the American South, and combined black blues with the country music of working class whites to produce a heavily rhythmic – "rocking" – sound that appealed especially to young people.

Many of rock and roll's first stars were black performers such as Chuck Berry and Little Richard. But the unchallenged "King" of rock-and-roll was a young southern white named Elvis Presley. In 1956 Presley's recordings were at the top of the American popularity list – the "hit parade" – every week from August to December. By the end of the decade he had become an international superstar.

To rock-and-roll enthusiasts, Presley came to symbolize a new culture of youth. Among other things, this culture developed its own vocabulary, ways of dressing, even hair styles. More significantly for the future, it began to reject socially approved ideas and ways of behaving.

By the 1970s rock-and-roll had blended with the protest songs of the 1960s to become rock, a music that was harder and less escapist. Rock became an international as well as an American phenomenon, one that millions of younger people worldwide saw as their natural cultural language. A large part of its appeal was that it symbolized opposition to officially approved ideas and standards even more strongly than its ancestor, rock-and-roll, had done in the 1950s.

The Americanization of popular taste and habits was not restricted to entertainment. The growing popularity of hamburgers, fried chicken and other easily prepared "fast food" spread American eating habits all over the world. Blue jeans and T-shirts Americanized the dress of people on every continent. And supermarkets Americanized the everyday experience of shopping for millions.

Elvis Presley, the "King" of rock-and-roll.

Fast food – McDonald's drive-in restaurant.

A supermarket in Texas.

The first supermarkets appeared in the United States in the 1950s. With their huge variety of foods and other consumer goods, supermarkets gave shoppers a much wider range of choices. In the 1950s many Americans saw their loaded shelves and full freezers as visible proof of the superiority of the American way of organizing a nation's economic life. Not surprisingly, when the Soviet leader Khrushchev visited the United States in 1959, one of the places he was taken to visit was a supermarket!

When supermarkets proved a commercial success in the United States they quickly spread to other prosperous countries, first in Europe and then in other parts of the world. So did another feature of American cities in these years – groups of tall, shining buildings with outer walls of glass and metal. By the 1980s such buildings were dominating city centers all over the world. To many people they were images of late-twentieth-century modernity. Yet their origins can be traced back more than a hundred years to the American Midwest.

During the 1880s a number of high, narrow buildings began to rise in the center of Chicago. Similar buildings – so tall that people called them "skyscrapers" – were soon rising over other American cities. In the first half of the twentieth century they became one of the principal visual symbols of the modern United States.

Skyscrapers were the result of a need for more working and living space in places where the cost of land was very high. Instead of using a lot of expensive space on the ground their builders used the free space of the sky. New industrial techniques, and the availability of plenty of cheap steel, made it possible for them to do this.

Each skyscraper was built around a framework of steel beams, or girders, which carried the weight of the building. This inner steel skeleton was constructed before the outer walls, which were added later. The walls of the early skyscrapers were often made of stone – not for practical reasons, but to make the buildings look solid and strong.

In the 1950s architects working in the United States began to design skyscrapers whose steel skeletons were covered by outer walls – or "curtains" – of glass and metal. One of the earliest examples was Mies van der Rohe and Philip Johnson's Seagram Building in New York. It was American buildings like this that inspired similar "glass box" office and apartment buildings in cities all over the world.

Such buildings gave visual expression to the impact of the United States on the twentieth-century world. They were gleaming symbols of a name that some historians were giving to the century even before it reached its end. The name was "the American Century."

The Seagram buiding in New York.

Additional information on illustrations

Page 5   *The Buffalo Hunt* by Charles M. Russell. Russell was a cowboy who taught himself to paint, and he became one of the best known artists of the American West. See also the painting on page 41.

Page 7   (T) Blackfoot Amerindian tepees painted by the German artist Karl Bodmer. In the 1830s Bodmer followed the route of the Lewis and Clark expedition across the Great Plains to the Rocky Mountains.

Page 7   (B) *Haida Indian Potlach* by Mort Künstler. This is a twentieth-century re-creation by Künstler who carries out detailed research to make his historical paintings as accurate as possible. See also paintings on pages 22, 30, 60 and 99.

Page 9   This is an Aztec drawing of an event in the Spanish conquest of Mexico during the expedition of Nuno de Guzman in 1530 when the Tlascalans aided the Spaniards in punishing another tribe which had hanged a Spaniard. The drawing is from the long-destroyed Lienzo de Tlascala canvas.

Page 17   A romanticized impression of the landing of the Pilgrim Fathers by a nineteenth-century artist.

Page 18   Pilgrims going to church painted by George H. Boughton in 1867.

Page 19   An impression of the first Thanksgiving by a nineteenth-century artist.

Page 20   A contemporary painting of Philadelphia by Peter Cooper.

Page 22   *Daniel Boone* by Mort Künstler (see notes to page 7).

Page 24   A contemporary engraving.

Page 26   (T) A contemporary English cartoon showing the burial of the Stamp Act. Written on the coffin are the words, "Born in 1765, Died in 1766."

Page 26   (B) An impression of the Boston Tea Party by a nineteenth-century artist.

Page 30   *Reading the Declaration of Independence to the Troops* by Mort Künstler (see notes to page 7).

Page 31   A contemporary portrait

Page 34   A contemporary painting by James Peale.

Page 36   An impression by a nineteenth-century artist.

Page 38   A contemporary painting.

Page 39   A contemporary engraving.

Page 41   *Indians Discovering Lewis and Clark* by Charles M. Russell (see notes to page 5).

Page 42   *Setting Traps for Beaver* by Alfred Jacob Miller. Miller sketched the Amerindians and mountain-men of the Rocky Mountains while traveling there in the 1830s.

Page 43   *When Wagon Trails were Dim* by Charles M. Russell (see notes to page 5).

Page 44   A contemporary nineteenth-century engraving.

Page 45   A contemporary nineteenth-century lithograph.

Page 46   A contemporary engraving.

Page 48   A contemporary portrait of Dred Scott by Louis Schulze.

Page 49   *The Underground Railroad* by Charles T. Webber. A contemporary nineteenth-century painting.

Page 54   A contemporary engraving.

Page 58   A contemporary engraving.

Page 60   *The Golden Spike* by Mort Künstler (see notes to page 7).

Page 61   *The Stampede* by Frederic Remington, painted in 1908. Remington spent many years painting and drawing in the American West. See also paintings on pages 63 and 68.

Page 63   (T) *Across the Continent. "Westward the Course of Empire Takes its Way"* by Fanny Palmer. An idealised hand-colored lithograph of the opening and settlement of the West (1868).

Page 63   (B)   *The Fall of the Cowboy* by Frederic Remington (see notes to page 61).

Page 65   A late nineteenth-century painting of Yellowstone National Park by Thomas Moran.

Page 67   An impression by a contemporary artist.

Page 68   *Ghost Dancers* by Frederic Remington (see notes to page 61). This painting of 1890 shows Ogallala Sioux performing the Ghost Dance at the Pine Ridge Indian Agency, South Dakota.

Page 76   *The Unveiling of the Statue of Liberty*. A contemporary painting by Francis G. Mayer.

Page 77   A hand-colored contemporary photograph.

Page 78   (T) An early twentieth-century photograph.

Page 78   (B) *Cliff Dwellers* by George Bellows.

Page 80   (B) A hand-colored photograph from the early 1900s.

Page 82   *The Strike* by Robert Koehler. The artist's representation of the tensions between labor and capital in the late nineteenth century.

Page 84   A contemporary print.

Page 86   A contemporary painting.

Page 88   A British propaganda poster making use of the sinking of the *Lusitania* in 1915 to arouse American sympathies.

Page 91   A contemporary painting by Sir William Orpen of the signing of the Versailles peace treaty.

Page 92   A magazine cover of 1926.

Page 99   *The Battle of Anacostia Flats* by Mort Künstler (see notes to page 7).

Page 122   A photograph of a section of the Berlin Wall covered with graffiti. The graffiti artist has painted a view of East Berlin through a skull-shaped hole in the wall.

INDEX

*need to include about the Religians →
　↳ Irish → Catholic
　↳ Blacks →
　↳ other Europeans　New"